OVERNIGHT MARKETING

How to Transform Your Business Overnight

DRU ARMITAGE

Contents

PART I

Overnight Marketing:

How to Transform Your Business Overnight

Are you looking for a way to change your business almost immediately? If so, then *Overnight Marketing* is the guidebook for you! This book explains how you can change your marketing and increase sales and traffic to your business overnight. The tips and advice in this book are easy to understand and implement, making it the perfect resource for businesses of all sizes. Whether you're a small business owner wanting to increase sales or a large corporation wanting to increase traffic, *Overnight Marketing* will provide you with the tools you need to make your business more successful. So, what are you waiting for?

Why Should You Read This Book

If you're like most business owners, you're always looking for ways to improve your business. You may have tried various marketing techniques, but you haven't seen the results you want. If this sounds familiar, then you need to read *Overnight Marketing*. This book differs from other marketing books because it provides specific, actionable advice you can implement immediately to see results. The tips in this book are easy to understand and implement, yet they are effective. In *Overnight Marketing*, you'll learn how to market your business to make it more successful overnight. You'll discover the benefits of marketing your business, as well as how to do it effectively. By the time you finish reading this book, you'll have all the tools you need to take your business to the next level.

The Benefits of Marketing Your Business Overnight

There are many benefits to marketing your business overnight. Perhaps the most obvious benefit is that you'll see an immediate increase in sales and traffic. However, there are other benefits as well.

By marketing your business overnight, you'll:

- Attract new customers and clients
- Increase brand awareness
- Generate more leads
- Boost online visibility

And much more

In addition, marketing your business overnight is a great way to get started if you're new to marketing. It's also an excellent way to jumpstart your marketing efforts if you've been struggling to see results.

Now that you know the benefits of marketing your business overnight, it's time to learn how to do it. Marketing your business doesn't have to be complicated or expensive.

How Do I Know This Book Is Right for You?

Well, if you're looking for an easy guide on how to change your business overnight, then this book is perfect for you. It's packed with valuable tips and insights that will help you immediately transform your business. Whether you're a small business owner or a large corporation, this book can help you increase sales and traffic to your business.

I know firsthand about making big decisions because let me tell you, after 10+ years working on autopilot mode without any real direction or passion behind anything I was doing, I was feeling stuck and frustrated. It took a lot of planning which I wasn't always great at, but after years of planning and writing this book, I decided to make the jump. I was employed for about a decade until I decided to open my own marketing agency.

Quitting my day job to start my marketing agency was one of the best decisions I've ever made. After years of corporate life, I realized that I wanted more than what the traditional workforce could offer me.

So, if you're feeling stagnant in your current position, or you're just not sure what you want to do with your life, don't be so quick to hand in your two weeks' notice! Instead, try exploring some other options first, like freelance work or looking at starting your own business. You never know what doors might open. The sky is the limit when it comes to starting your own business. You can be anything you want to be and do anything you set your mind to. You may have the opportunity at some point in time to pursue your passions and explore other opportunities outside of traditional employment. But with great power comes great responsibility, and with entrepreneurship comes a lot of hard work.

But what if there was a way to make the process of starting your business a little bit easier? What if there was a way to transform your business overnight, without having to put in all the extra time and effort?

The old saying is true: if you do the same thing over and over and expect a different result, then insanity lies in store for your efforts. This could not be more applicable to business than with marketing. There are so many people who believe they're lucky because their video went viral on YouTube or Facebook and recently TikTok—when all they needed was one good promotion in film (with proper planning) to get their product out into front of thousands of potential customers! The truth about success though? It's not just luck that successful people have; it comes from working hard day after day, even when it feels like you're putting in more effort than anyone else and getting nowhere. Your dedication will pay off eventually, while others might give up too soon. So, if you're looking for a way to improve your business overnight, then this book is definitely worth a read.

How To Read This Book

As you read, remember that the book is a quick, easy read. The tips and advice are meant to be implemented right away, so you can see results overnight. However, don't do everything at once—start with one or two changes, and then add more as you go. You want to first start by reading this book front to back to understand the concepts and terms associated if you are unfamiliar with them. Then, you can revert to a chapter you would like a refresher on. The idea is to keep this book handy next to you at all times.

The first step is to identify the areas of your business where you could make a change. Are you not getting enough website traffic? Are your sales down? Are customers not returning? Once you've identified the areas that need improvement, the next step is to make a plan of action. This book provides a variety of tips and techniques to help increase your business's success. However, not all of these tips will work for every business. You need to find the techniques that are most relevant to your business and use them to create your own marketing strategy.

One of the most important things to remember is that marketing is an ongoing process. You can't simply implement a few changes and then forget about it—you must continue to work on your marketing strategy to see results. Don't get discouraged if you don't see an immediate increase in sales or traffic; keep at it, and eventually you will see results. The opportunity to market your business overnight is one that should not be missed. By following the tips and advice in this book, you can change your business almost immediately and see a difference in sales and traffic. The information in this book is insightful and easy to understand, making it a valuable resource for anyone looking to market their business more successfully. Whether you're a small business owner or a large corporation, this book can help you see an increase in sales and traffic overnight. Don't miss your chance to read some helpful insights!

By following my advice, you can increase sales and traffic to your business almost immediately. And best of all, my techniques are easy to understand and implement. So, if you're looking to change your business, *Overnight Marketing* is the perfect guidebook.

Why Should You Believe in Me?

As an expert in marketing with over 10 years of experience, I created a successful agency by myself with little financial risk while replacing my income from my 9-5 position within less than one month! I not only hold two degrees, including a bachelor's in psychology and a master's degree in industrial/organizational psychology, but I have also written this book that provides valuable tips on how you can see overnight success. This isn't to say that business owners who didn't go to school are any less successful. This book seeks to improve your business overnight without any false hype or unnecessary nonsense.

If you're not constantly evolving your marketing strategy, you'll quickly fall behind. That's why I wrote this book - to provide valuable tips on how you can see overnight success. Don't miss out on this great chance to improve your understanding and implementation skills! I share all these tips inside *Overnight Marketing*, which provides those tips and advice that are valuable. If you want to see an influx of traffic and sales on your website, this is something you can't afford to miss!

Marketing has always been one of the key pillars of success for any business. But in today's fast-paced world, it's more important than ever to stay ahead of the competition. Businesses that don't innovate soon become defunct. If you're not progressing, you will begin to lose ground.

Overnight Marketing will show you how to make the changes you need to stay ahead of the curve. With my help, I can transform your business almost immediately.

By utilizing social media for marketing, businesses have seen an astounding increase of more than half in sales! That's right—if you're not marketing on social media, you're missing out on a huge chunk of potential sales. So, what are you waiting for? Start marketing on social media today and see the difference it makes.

After establishing an ad campaign strategy for a company, I have seen traffic grow by at least 35%. This is due to the vast reach that social media platforms have and the ability to specifically target your audience with laser precision.

Believe there is no such thing as overnight success—it takes years of hard work and dedication to become successful. However, believe that by marketing your business overnight, you can change your fortunes almost immediately.

Believe that you can change your business overnight by marketing it in the right way. This belief will help you to focus on the task at hand and see the potential for success hiding in plain sight.

Marketing your business overnight can be a game changer. You can make small changes that will result in large differences for your company. Sometimes it only takes a little effort to make a big impact.

This Book Is for You...

This book is for business owners of all sizes who want to increase their sales and traffic. This book provides valuable tips on how to market your business in a way that is easy to understand and implement and will help you see success overnight. Whether you're just starting out, a small business owner, or a large corporation, this book has something to offer you.

This Book Is Not For...

If you aren't willing to put in the effort, this book won't be useful to you. The strategies here take both dedication and time before you'll see results. If what you want is a quick solution with no work required, look elsewhere. Only those willing to put in the effort can see success from following the advice in *Overnight Marketing*.

This book is perfect for anyone who wants to change their business quickly and efficiently.

However, it is up to the reader to put in the hard work required to make these changes successful.

- Are you tired of having no online presence?
- Do you struggle to generate leads and sales online?

Are you ready for immediate changes in your business, overnight?

Skeptics Read This...

A skeptical person would question how effective *Overnight Marketing* can be. They would argue that it takes time and effort to build a successful business and that overnight marketing cannot possibly make a significant impact. They would also claim that any success achieved through overnight marketing is likely due to luck and not the marketing tactics used.

No matter your what your business is, if you are not doing any marketing, you are not reaching your full potential. Even if you think you are doing well and do not need to change anything, this book can show you how to market your business to make it more successful overnight. So, whether you think your business is perfect or not, this book can help you to take it to the next level.

How This Book Is Unique

Overnight Marketing is unique from other books on the sub-ject because it provides an easy-to-follow guide that is both insightful and witty. *Overnight Marketing* is unlike other books that simply provide readers with a dry, step-by-step instruction manual on how to market their business. This book provides real-life examples of businesses that have increased sales and traffic by following the advice within its pages.

This book is also different because it does not just focus on marketing your business, but on changing little things about your business that can make a big difference. This includes ev-erything from changing your website design to improving your customer service.

Overall, this book differs from other books on the subject by implementing specific strategies and techniques that can be used to start your own business. It also provides helpful advice for those who are considering making a career change. If you are looking for a way to start your own business, this book is a great resource.

What Are 4 Ways This Book Differs from Others?

1. *Overnight Marketing* is written in a fun and easy-to-understand way while still providing valuable insights on how to market your business overnight. This book is perfect for those who are considering making a career change and starting their own business, as it provides helpful advice for getting started with your own venture in terms of marketing online.

2. This book is full of clever and perceptive tips on how to make your business more successful overnight.

   - How to create a marketing plan that works for your business
   - How to use social media to increase traffic to your business
   - How to use online advertising to increase sales for your business
   - Why SEO is important for your business

3. This book provides valuable information on how to make small changes that will have a big impact on your business's marketing.

Some valuable information that can help businesses make small changes to increase their success overnight include:

- Creating a marketing plan specific to your business and its needs
- Using social media to connect with customers and promote your products or services

4. This book is up to date with the latest trends in marketing, so you can be sure you're using the most effective techniques.

Looking to stay ahead of the competition? Check out our latest marketing trends and discover how you can use them to your advantage. From social media to online advertising, we have all the information you need to make your business more successful overnight.

1. What are the fundamental principles of marketing?

2. *Overnight Marketing* is geared towards businesses of all sizes, from small businesses looking to increase sales, to large corporations wanting to increase traffic.

3. *Overnight Marketing* provides valuable tips on how to market your business in a way that is both successful and witty.

4. This book is an easy and fast read, giving you the information you need to start marketing your business overnight.

I've always been intrigued by marketing, but I felt lost on where to start. So, over the last decade, I started reading books about marketing and how to increase traffic. Books and self-learning through my experiences taught me everything I needed to know about marketing my business successfully overnight.

Overnight Marketing: How to Transform Your Business Overnight

- Understand the basics of overnight marketing
- Know your target audience
- Create a slogan or catchphrase for your business
- Use social media to market your business
- Make a website for your business
- Use search engine optimization to increase traffic to your website
- Advertise your business offline and online
- Give customers reasons to return to your business
- Celebrate milestones and track progress

PART II

Chapter 1

Introduction

What are the biggest problems businesses have with marketing today?

The biggest problem businesses have with marketing is that it's difficult to know where to start. There are so many options available, and it can be overwhelming to decide what will be most effective for your business. Additionally, many businesses struggle with maintaining a consistent marketing plan, which can lead to inconsistency in results. Marketing is essential for any business to reach new customers and grow. With so many options available, it's difficult to know which type of marketing will be most effective for your business.

However, by using a variety of marketing strategies, you can increase your chances of reaching more customers and growing your business. Additionally, maintaining a consistent marketing plan is essential for achieving long-term success.

- What are the biggest problem businesses have with marketing today

- Why is it important to use marketing for your business today
- How can you create a successful marketing plan
- What is the most effective marketing
- How can you measure the success of your marketing efforts
- What are common mistakes made in marketing
- How can you stay up to date with the latest trends in marketing
- How can you use technology to improve your marketing
- What are ethical considerations to remember when marketing
- How can you transform your business almost immediately with the power of marketing

To create a successful marketing plan, many businesses find marketing to be a daunting task because of the sheer number of options available. Many businesses find it difficult to stick with one marketing strategy, which then leads to an overall lack of consistent results.

What is the biggest problem businesses have with marketing today?

The biggest problem businesses have with marketing is that it's difficult to know where to start. With so many options available, it can be tough to determine what will work best for your business. Also, many businesses find it difficult to keep up with a regular marketing plan, which often leads them to see little-to-no ROI (return on investment).

Why is it important to use marketing for your business today?

Marketing is essential for any business to reach new customers and grow. With so many options available, it's difficult to know which type of marketing will be most effective for your specific business. However, by using a variety of marketing strategies, you can increase your chances of reaching more customers and growing your business. Additionally, maintaining a consistent marketing plan is essential for achieving long-term success.

How can you create a successful marketing plan?

To create a successful marketing plan, understand the biggest problem isn't just the inconsistencies of marketing with different options, but effectively managing these consistencies. Furthermore, if your marketing strategy isn't cohesive, it'll be difficult to produce stable results.

However, by using a variety of marketing strategies, you can increase your chances of reaching more customers and growing your business. Plans change, but a good marketing strategy always adapts and eventually leads to success.

Here are four steps you can take to create a successful marketing plan:

- Define your goals—What do you want to achieve with your marketing efforts?

- Choose the right channels for reaching your target audience
- Create compelling content that engages your audience
- Measure the success of your marketing efforts and make necessary adjustments

By following these steps, you can create a successful marketing plan that will help you reach more customers and grow your business.

What are the most effective types of marketing?

There are many types of marketing, but some of the most effective include online marketing, social media marketing, content marketing, email marketing, and search engine optimization (SEO). By using a variety of marketing, you can reach more potential customers and grow your business. For marketing your business, it's important to use a variety of strategies to reach the most potential customers.

Online marketing is any type of marketing that takes place over the internet. This can include things like website design and development, online advertising, email marketing, and social media marketing. By using online marketing strategies, you can reach more people in a shorter amount of time and often for less money than traditional marketing methods. Social media marketing involves using social networking sites like Facebook, Twitter, LinkedIn, and Google+ to promote your business.

By creating interesting and engaging content and by interacting with your followers and customers on these sites, you can build a strong social media presence for your business. This can help you attract new customers and keep existing customers engaged with your business. Content marketing is creating and publishing content relevant to your target market. This can include blog posts, articles, e-books, white papers, webinars, videos, and infographics. By creating valuable content interesting to your target market, you can attract new customers and keep them returning for more.

Email marketing is sending targeted emails to your customer base. These emails can be used to promote new products or services, announce special offers or discounts, or simply keep your customers up to date on what's going on with your business. Email marketing is a cost-effective way to reach many people with your message.

How can you measure the success of your marketing efforts?

There are a variety of ways to measure the success of your marketing efforts. One way is to track the number of leads or sales you generate through your campaigns. Another measure of success is by looking at engagement metrics such as website visits, social media shares or likes, and email opens or clicks. By tracking these metrics, you can get a better idea of what is working and what needs to be improved.

If you're not sure where to start, here are a few tips for measuring the effectiveness of your marketing campaigns:

- Track the number of leads or sales you generate from each campaign. This will better show you which campaigns are most effective in generating revenue.

- Analyze engagement metrics such as website visits, social media shares or likes, and email opens or clicks. This will help you determine which channels are most effective in engaging your target audience.
- Compare your results against your goals and objectives. If you're not meeting your targets, then it's time to adjust your marketing plan.

Make use of analytics tools to track the performance of your campaigns. This will help you identify trends and make necessary changes to keep up with the competition.

One way to measure the success of your marketing efforts is to track how many leads or sales you generate because of your campaigns. By tracking these metrics, you can get a better idea of what is working and what needs to be improved.

What are common mistakes made in marketing?

One common mistake made in marketing is not tracking results. Without tracking the results of your campaigns, you won't know which ones are successful and which ones need improvement. Failing to adjust your marketing plan based on your results can lead to failure. Another common mistake is not targeting the right audience. If you're not reaching the right people with your message, you're not going to see the results you want.

Failing to create valuable content is another mistake often made in marketing. If your content isn't interesting or valuable to your target market, they won't engage with it. And finally, not using the right channels can also lead to ineffective marketing.

Choosing the wrong social media platforms or email service providers can limit your reach and impact.

How can you stay up to date with the latest trends in marketing?

One way to stay up to date with the latest trends in marketing is to subscribe to industry newsletters. This will give you a weekly or monthly overview of the latest news and trends in your industry. Following industry blogs and attending industry events can help you stay up to date with the latest developments.

How can you use technology to improve your marketing?

Technology can play a major role in improving your marketing efforts. By using the latest tools and technologies, you can improve your reach, engagement, and effectiveness. Here are a few ways that technology can help:

- Use your social media platforms to reach a wider audience.
- Use email service providers to reach a larger number of people with your message.
- Track the results of your campaigns using analytics tools.
- Create valuable content that engages your target market.
- By using technology, you can improve your chances of reaching more people with your message and seeing better results from your campaigns.

What are ethical considerations to remember when marketing?

When marketing, it is important to keep in mind the ethical considerations of your actions. Here are a few things to keep in mind:

- Make sure you are truthful and accurate in your advertising. Do not make false or misleading claims about your product or service.
- Make sure you are respectful of your customers and do not spam them with unwanted advertising.
- Do not use unethical methods to promote your product or service, such as deceptive pricing or bait-and-switch tactics.
- By keeping these ethical considerations in mind, you can ensure that your marketing campaigns are honest and respectful of your customers.

How can you transform your business almost immediately with the power of marketing?

If you're looking to take your business to the next level, marketing is the key. By using the power of marketing, you can reach a wider audience and generate more leads and sales. Marketing can help you create valuable content that engages your target market and using the latest technology can help improve your results.

Marketing can be a complex process, but by understanding the basics, you can create successful campaigns that reach your target market. In this chapter, we discussed some of the most common mistakes made in marketing. Failing to track results, not targeting the right audience, and not creating valuable content are just a few of the mistakes that can lead to failure.

Additionally, it is important to keep in mind the ethical considerations of marketing. By being truthful and respectful to your customers, you can ensure that your marketing campaigns are honest and successful. We looked at how technology can help improve your marketing efforts. By harnessing the power of technology, you expand your potential audience and campaign reach, leading to improved results. Marketing is a significant investment for any business owner who wants to see their company reach new heights.

If you're looking to take your business to the next level, don't hesitate to invest in marketing. It could be the best decision you ever make.

Chapter 2
Growing Pains with Marketing

The problem we are solving is how to transform your business almost immediately by marketing and changing little things to increase sales and traffic to your business. Oftentimes, business transformations seem much more difficult than they need to be because we don't take the time to understand them. We must start with the basics, like setting goals and understanding our target audience. If we understand these two things, then we can create a successful plan for marketing that will work and get us the results we want.

- Introducing the concept of overnight marketing
- What is needed to change for your business to succeed overnight
- How to apply overnight marketing techniques in a way that is effective for your business

The problem we are solving is how to transform your business almost immediately by marketing and changing little things to increase sales and traffic to your business. We will provide tips on how to change a way that is witty and insightful yet easy to understand and implement.

Action Step 1: The first step is understanding the problem and what needs to change for your business to succeed overnight. Action Step 2: Next, you need to learn about the concept of *Overnight Marketing* and what makes it so successful. Action

Step 3: After that, download our free eBook, which provides valuable tips on how you can apply *Overnight Marketing* techniques in a way that is effective for your business. Action Step 4: Once you have read through this book, implement the techniques into your business plan. Remember, not everything will work for everyone, so find the strategies that fit best with what you are trying to achieve. Action Step 5: Track your progress! Keep track of what works and what doesn't as you go along so you can make necessary adjustments along the way.

Now that you understand creativity is inherent in all of us, it's time to break the bad habits preventing you from expressing your unique perspective.

Which of these habits is holding you back from success the most?

- Procrastination
- Perfectionism
- Analysis paralysis
- Fear of failure
- Fear of success
- Impostor syndrome

- Comparisonitis
- Negativity

Once you've identified which bad habits are holding you back the most, it's time to work on breaking them. Again, this is where a growth mindset comes in handy. Here are tips for breaking each bad habit:

- Procrastination: If you procrastinate, it may help to set smaller goals or deadlines. You can also try breaking down a larger goal into smaller steps you can complete. Additionally, it may help to establish a specific time each day when you will work towards your goal.

- Perfectionism: If you are a perfectionist, it's important to remember no one is perfect. Try to focus on the progress you've made rather than dwelling on mistakes. Additionally, it's helpful to set realistic goals for yourself.

- Analysis paralysis: If you get bogged down in details, try to step back and focus on the big picture. Once you have a general plan, you can fill in the details. Additionally, it may help to set a deadline for yourself, so you don't get too caught up in the planning process.

- Fear of failure: If you're afraid of failing, it's important to remember that everyone makes mistakes. What matters is how you learn from your mistakes and move forward. To stay on track, set aside a specific time each day to work towards your goal.

- Fear of success: If you're afraid of succeeding, it may help to think about what success would mean for you and your life. Additionally, it may help to set small goals at first and you can gradually build up to bigger ones.

- Impostor syndrome: If you feel like a fraud or impostor, it's important to remember that everyone feels this way. What matters is how you handle these feelings and move forward. Additionally, it may help to read about or talk to others who have experienced impostor syndrome.

- Comparisonitis: If you are constantly comparing yourself to others, it can be difficult to stay focused on your own goals. Instead of looking at what others have done, try to focus on what you want to achieve. Remember, you are unique, and no one can do things exactly the way you do.

- Negativity: If you are negative, it's important to focus on the positive. Additionally, it may help to surround yourself with positive people who can help support you.

By following these steps and breaking these bad habits, you will be well on your way to increasing sales and traffic to your business almost immediately! These changes are easy to understand and implement, so wait no longer.

Now that you have read about the introduction of *Overnight Marketing*, the concept behind it, and how to apply it in a way relevant to your business, it's time for action. Here are steps you can take to get started:

- Understand the problem we are solving and how overnight marketing can help solve it
- Identify what needs to change for your business to succeed overnight
- Learn about the techniques involved in *Overnight Marketing* and select those that will work best for your company
- Implement these changes and track the results over time
- Celebrate your success! Overnight marketing can be an effective way to transform your business quickly and easily. If you follow these steps, success in marketing will come to you more quickly than you thought possible.

Chapter 3
Your Method for Creating this Change

Why is the *Overnight Marketing* method different? One of the unique methods for solving the *Overnight Marketing* problem is through change. Most businesses only make small incremental changes which can take months or years to have an impact. Marketing overnight introduces a new way of thinking that can help to change your business almost immediately.

- Understand the overnight marketing method
- Why change is essential for overnight success
- Learn how to make changes quickly and effectively
- Use change to your advantage to beat the competition
- Implement overnight marketing strategies for your business
- Monitor results and adjust as necessary

To make these changes, you must first understand the overnight marketing method. This involves understanding why change is essential for overnight success and learning to make changes quickly and effectively. You can then use change to your advantage to beat the competition and implement overnight marketing strategies for your business. Finally, monitor results and adjust to continue achieving success with this approach.

Since we now understand that everyone has the ability to be creative, it's time to learn how to harness that power.

Stop being a perfectionist in terms of creativity

The quest for perfection is the enemy of creativity. When you're too focused on getting things just right, you miss out on opportunities to try new things and explore different possibilities. Instead of striving for perfection, focus on progress. Experimentation is key to innovation, so embrace your inner scientist and allow yourself to fail.

Break the rules

If you always play by the rules, you'll never discover new territory. To be creative, you need to be willing to color outside the lines and think outside the box. So break some rules! Make sure you're not breaking any laws.

Be open-minded

Creativity requires an open mind. If you're too closed off to new ideas, you'll never be able to generate original thoughts of your own. Instead of being quick to judge, try to be open to all possibilities. You never know where a great idea might come from.

Be persistent

Giving up too soon is a surefire way to kill your creativity. When you encounter a problem or obstacle, don't give up—find a way around it. And if you can't find a solution right away, keep brainstorming until you do. There's no such thing as an unsolvable problem—only people who stop trying too soon.

Take risks

To be creative, you must be willing to take risks. That means stepping out of your comfort zone and trying something new. It might be scary at first, but it's also the only way to discover something original.

Be flexible

Rigidity is the enemy of creativity. If you're too set in your ways, you'll never be able to adapt to change or come up with new ideas. Instead, learn to go with the flow and be open to new possibilities. Prepare to change course on a moment's notice as things rarely go as expected. Being flexible and open-minded are essential traits for anyone looking to increase their creativity.

Be open to change

Be willing to try new things. Experimentation is key to innovation, so don't be afraid to break out of your comfort zone. Be patient. It takes time and practice to develop flexibility and open-mindedness. Don't give up if it takes a while to see results. Being too rigid can come at a price, such as not hearing your employees give you constructive feedback on how customers are behaving toward a new process. It doesn't have to be rocket science; we sometimes tend to overcomplicate things as managers when our staff are the ones that are out in the trenches serving the customers. By getting your employee's feedback, you open yourself to being flexible and open-minded when looking for new ideas. Remember, just because that person is your subordinate doesn't mean they don't have a million-dollar idea.

Stimulate your mind

To be more creative, you need to keep your mind active and engaged. That means regularly challenging yourself with new ideas and problems to solve. Reading, learning new things, and taking on new hobbies are all great ways to keep your mind sharp.

Get some sleep

Sleep is often overlooked as a crucial time for creativity, but it plays an essential role in restoring your mind and body. A good night's sleep isn't just important for your physical health—it can also improve your mental clarity and help you to come up with new ideas. So, make sure to get plenty of rest, your creativity will thank you! If you want to be more creative, aim to think differently and come up with novel concepts.

I always thought that getting too much sleep was bad, but not getting enough sleep is far worse. Make sure to figure out what works best for you. I am 100% a night owl when it comes to working, that is my excuse as to why I sleep in till 8 am. Figure out what works best for you, not what others say works best for them.

One of the most important things you can do is get some sleep. When you're well-rested, your mind is clear, and you're better able to think creatively.

For example, can you recall a time when you had to come up with an original solution quickly? Maybe you were working on a project and ran into a roadblock. Or maybe you were at a meeting, and someone came up with a suggestion that you hadn't thought of. In either case, you had to be creative and come up with a solution quickly. I remember trying to always be the smartest guy in the room, the first to talk, the first to think of an extremely clever idea, and wanted to be praised instantly for my idea. Remember to check your ego at the door before you enter that group of other people it will improve your thoughts and ideas when you're in a group setting.

You can also look to others for inspiration. Ask your team, colleagues, or other professionals what they do to stay creative and get ideas. You might be surprised at how different every-one's approach is and the fantastic suggestions you get from simply asking around! And lastly, don't forget to have fun! It doesn't have to be a fight on who has the best ideas. A collaborative environment can produce great results. It doesn't have to be a stressful situation; enjoy the process and you will see much better outcomes. So go ahead and challenge yourself with new ideas and problems to solve.

Now that you've read this chapter, it's time to take some action. Pick one or two of the tips and put them into practice. See how they work for you and make changes as needed. Remember that overnight marketing is an ongoing process. Always be looking for new ways to improve your business and increase sales. Furthermore, don't forget to keep track of your progress so you can measure results and continue to improve. Keep a journal of what you do, what works, and what doesn't so you can refer to it later on. Remember to celebrate your success-es! Share them with us on social media or our blog so we can applaud your hard work.

Chapter 4

What Does Your Business Represent?

To be successful, your business needs to represent something that people can connect with. It needs to have a message that people can get behind, and it needs to be something that people want to be a part of. You need to make sure that you're portraying the right image, and you need to make sure that your message is clear.

When thinking about what your business represents, try asking yourself a few questions. What is the message that you're trying to send? What are you trying to accomplish? And most importantly, what do you want people to think about your business? When you have a strong message and a clear vision, it will be much easier to market your business correctly.

Businesses aren't just about making money. They're about representing something bigger than themselves. Whether it's a product, a service, or a cause, businesses have the opportunity to stand for something and make a difference in the world.

This all starts with marketing. Businesses need to communicate what they represent in a way that resonates with their target audience. Only then can they hope to make a lasting impact. What does your business represent? That's for you to decide. As you go about your work, always remember that it's not solely about making a profit; consider how you can positively affect change.

The most important thing is to stay true to yourself and your values. When you stand for something, it will be much easier for people to connect with you. Make sure that your message is authentic, and make sure that you're proud of what your business represents.

- What does your business represent?
- Why is it important to stay true to yourself and your values?
- How can you make sure that your message is clear?
- What are the most important things to consider when marketing your business

Special Tip: Place Your Business in the Right Light

As a business owner, you always want to make sure that your establishment is well lit. This is one of the first things potential customers will notice when they walk in. If your store or office is dim, it can make people feel uncomfortable and less likely to want to stay and browse or conduct business. Good lighting makes a space feel more open, inviting, and positive. Not only does this make it more aesthetically pleasing, but it also allows people to see what they're looking for more easily. There are a few things you can do to make sure your business is properly lit:

- Make sure all bulbs are working and at full capacity. This may seem like a no-brainer, but you'd be surprised how often businesses have dim or flickering lights. This can make your space seem outdated and unkempt.

- Take advantage of natural light. If your business has large windows, open the curtains or blinds during the day to let in sunlight. This will not only help improve the look of your space, but it will also cut down on your energy costs.

- Use accent lighting. In addition to general lighting, you can use accent lighting to highlight certain areas or products in your store. This can be a great way to draw attention to sales or special items.

- Invest in quality lighting fixtures. Cheap fixtures can make your whole space look cheap and poorly made. Investing in higher quality fixtures will make a big difference to the overall look and feel of your business.

- Get creative with lighting if you want to make a statement. This could mean using different colors, patterns, or even lights that move or change color. Be careful not to overdo it, though, as this can be off putting to customers.

A great way to add some spice to your business' lighting is by choosing light fixtures that match well with your office or place of business. For example, if you have a modern, minimalist office, try using sleek, modern light fixtures. If you have a more traditional office, try using light fixtures with a classic look. You can also use light fixtures to match the theme of your business. If you own a restaurant, for example, you might want to use fixtures that resemble candles or chandeliers. This will create a more inviting and romantic atmosphere for your guests. I know you wouldn't want to go into a place of business that doesn't portray what they're selling.

The most important thing for businesses to remember is that they need to indicate what they represent in a way that resonates with their target audience. Only then can they hope to make a lasting impact. So, what does your business represent? That's for you to decide. But however, you answer that question, remember that it's not just about making a quick buck. It's also about making a difference.

Make sure that your message is authentic, and make sure that you're proud of what your business represents. And don't forget to place your business in the right light! Make sure all bulbs are working and at full capacity, take advantage of natural light, use accent lighting, and invest in quality lighting fixtures. Get creative with your lighting, and make sure it compliments the style of your office or place of business.

By following these tips, you can ensure that your business is well-lit and inviting to customers. Proper lighting can make a big difference in the overall look and feel of your space, and it can help increase sales and foot traffic.

Now that you know how to change your business almost immediately with marketing and changing some aspects of your business it's time to get started! Remember to take things one step at a time so you don't get overwhelmed. If you ever have questions, our team at *Overnight Marketing* is always here to help.

Chapter 5

Get More Customers in the Door

There are many ways to market your business, and what works for one company might not work for another. However, there are a few basic marketing principles that always work, no matter what the product or service is. In this chapter, we'll discuss some of the most effective overnight marketing techniques you can use to transform your business almost immediately.

- The different methods of overnight marketing
- Discuss the importance of getting more customers in the door
- Offer tips on how to attract more customers
- Explain how to convert your leads into paying customers

One of the simplest and most effective overnight marketing techniques is to create a strong branding strategy. Branding is all about creating a unique identity for your company that sets you apart from the competition. This can be done through logos, slogans, colors, and other visual elements. You can also use eye-catching graphics and images to draw people's attention to your website or storefront. Platforms such as Facebook, Twitter, and Instagram can help you to extend your marketing messages' reach. It's important to make sure that your branding is consistent across all channels, including your website, social media profiles, and advertising materials.

Your website is your business' mouth on the internet. If you don't make an effort to optimize it, people will find out more easily what's going on inside. By including these rich media types in your website, you'll not only have more opportunities for people to see you'll site, but also a chance that you'll search results page will rank higher. If your website isn't SEO friendly, it may not show up in search results at all. This means that potential customers who are looking for you or your services won't even know you exist. In other words, no visibility equals zero business and no money coming in.

If you don't have a website that is SEO friendly, you will miss out on a lot of potential customers. In order to compete in today's online marketplace, it's essential to have a strong online presence. This includes a website, blog, and social media profiles. By having feeds from your social media profiles that directly link to your website, you can easily stay up to date on what is new. Lastly, social media shouldn't be overlooked. Platforms such as Facebook, Twitter and LinkedIn provide a great opportunity to connect with possible consumers and create brand awareness. By sharing quality content and interacting with people who follow you online, you can not only increase brand awareness but also generate sales leads. As a business owner, you know that one of the most important things you can do is get more customers in the door. But how do you do that? Well, one of the best ways to bring in more customers is to market your business to capture their attention. And one of the best ways to do that is by using clever marketing techniques that will make your business more successful overnight.

A common misconception is that only smart people can be creative. Although it is commonly believed that intelligence and creativity are linked, I have seen some highly intelligent people who lacked in terms of creativity. Don't be discouraged and think that only smart people can be artistic. Most people have the potential to be highly creative, but they often develop habits that crush their creativity. These habits can be broken if you're willing to put in the effort. Leverage social media platforms such as Facebook, Instagram and YouTube to reach a larger audience. Make sure that your branding is consistent across all channels—website, social profiles, etc. Here are some of those habits and how to break them:

Habit 1: Not Asking "What If?"

The first habit that stifles creativity is failing to ask, "what if?" When you encounter a problem, the natural tendency is to find a solution that has worked in the past. But that's not always the best approach. Instead, try asking, "what if?" What if there were a different way to solve this problem? What if I looked at it from a different perspective? By asking "what if," you open yourself up to new possibilities and solutions.

Habit 2: Being Afraid to Fail

The second habit that stifles creativity is being afraid to fail. Since we were young, society has instilled the importance of success in our minds. And while that's true, it's also important to fail. Because when we fail, we learn what doesn't work, and we can try something else. The key is not to fear failing. Embrace it as a necessary step on the road to success. I strongly believe that if your original plan doesn't work, don't make a new one. Just reevaluate your original plan. Because in the back of your mind you will think that if this doesn't work, I'll do this instead. If you're constantly worrying about failing, you're not setting yourself up for success. Instead, adopt a sink-or-swim mentality and use failure as motivation to keep going.

Habit 3: Being Too Focused

The third habit that stifles creativity is being too focused. When you're too focused on one thing, you miss other possibilities. It's important to step back and look at the big picture. Try to see the problem from different angles and consider all the options. Only then will you be able to find the best solution.

Habit 4: Being a Perfectionist

The fourth habit that stifles creativity is being a perfectionist. Perfectionism is the enemy of creativity because it means you're never satisfied with your ideas. You're always looking for ways to make them better. But the fact is, there's no such thing as a perfect idea. The sooner you accept that, the sooner you can move on and create something great.

Habit 5: Being Too Analytical

The fifth and final habit that stifles creativity is being too analytical. When you're too analytical, you overthink things and try to find the perfect solution. But sometimes the best solutions are the simplest ones. Sometimes the best way to solve a problem is to take a leap of faith and go with your gut.

If you can break these five habits, you'll open yourself up to a world of possibilities. You'll find it easier to come up with creative solutions to problems. And you'll be well on your way to becoming a more creative person. Stop caring about the opinions of others and have faith in yourself that you will reach your goals no matter what.

Finally, you can also use traditional marketing methods to get new customers in the door. This includes advertising on social media platforms and even some traditional methods that still work such as the radio and newspaper (if still applicable), or on TV. While these methods may not be as effective as some of the other methods mentioned above, they're still worth considering if you want to reach a wide audience.

Marketing your business doesn't have to be difficult, it's time to take advantage of this knowledge! To get started, here are a few simple steps:

- Evaluate your current marketing strategy and see where there may be room for improvement.
- Identify what new methods or techniques you want to try based on what we've discussed in this book.

One way to identify new methods or techniques is to look at what your competition is doing. See what's working for them and try to adapt those methods for your own business. You can also look at what's popular in the industry right now and try to incorporate those trends into your marketing strategy. Get creative and come up with your own ideas that no one else is doing. The possibilities are endless, it all depends on what you're comfortable with trying.

- Start small and test out these new methods gradually; don't make any rash decisions that could hurt your business.

- Track the results of your new marketing efforts so you can gauge their effectiveness and make necessary adjustments along the way.

- Celebrate your successes (and learn from your failures) as you continue your journey to *Overnight Marketing* success!

- Start by creating a social media profile for your business, if you haven't already done so. This is a great way to connect with potential customers and promote your products or services.

Step by Step to Creating a Facebook Profile/Page:

To create a Facebook profile for your business, go to Facebook. com and click the "Create a Page" button. Choose the type of business you have and click "Get Started." Enter the required information and click "Create Profile."

Upload a profile photo and cover photo and add some information about your business.

Add a link to your website and start posting updates about your business on Facebook.

- If you have a website, make sure it's optimized for search engines so potential customers can find you online.

- Consider using paid advertising methods such as Google AdWords or Facebook Ads to reach more people quickly.

- Finally, continue learning about marketing and stay up to date on the latest trends so you can keep your business ahead of the competition.

Chapter 6
Increase Traffic to Your Business

Traffic is the lifeblood of any business. No matter how great your product or service is, if no one knows about it, you will not succeed. This chapter provides you with tips and tactics on how to increase traffic to your business.

One of the best ways to increase traffic is to create a strong online presence. This means having a website, blog, and social media profiles that are well-designed and up to date. Include keywords in your website and social media content that people are likely to search for.

Another great way to increase traffic is to offer something of value for free. This could be a white paper, e-book, or report. People are more likely to visit your website if they know they will get something out of it.

- The importance of having a strong online presence
- How to create a website, blog, and social media profiles
- Keywords to include in your content

- Offering something of value for free
- Tactics for increasing traffic through social media

Furthermore, create relationships with other businesses in your field. This can be done by guest blogging, attending trade shows, or joining industry associations. By networking with other businesses, you will not only increase traffic to your own website but also create valuable relationships that can benefit your business in the long run.

Once you have new customers coming in the door, you need to make sure they keep coming back. One way to do this is to increase traffic to your business. This can be done in several ways, but one of the most effective is by optimizing your website for search engines. This will ensure that when people search for businesses like yours, yours will be one of the first they see. There are several ways to do this, but one of the most effective is by using keyword-rich titles and descriptions. You can also use social media to draw attention to your business and drive traffic to your website. Finally, you can also increase traffic through paid advertising. Paid advertising allows you to target specific audiences with ads that appear on websites and in search engine results pages. There are several types of paid advertising, such as Google AdWords, Facebook Ads, and LinkedIn Ads.

One of the most effective is by utilizing social media. Social media allows you to connect with potential customers and have them become a part of your business's success. Social media platforms, such as Facebook, Twitter and LinkedIn are a fun way to connect with potential customers and promote your businesses. Depending on your business goals, some social media platforms may be more advantageous than others.

Facebook is a great platform for connecting with customers on a personal level. You can create pages for your business and post updates about new products or services, special offers, or just share interesting content that will engage your audience. You can also run ads on Facebook, which allows you to target specific audiences with ads that appear on their newsfeeds.

Twitter is great for promoting your business in real-time. You can tweet about upcoming events, new products, or special promotions. You can also run ads on Twitter, which allows you to target specific audiences with ads that appear in their Twitter feeds.

LinkedIn is a great platform for promoting your business to other businesses. You can create profiles for your business and connect with other businesses in your industry. You can also post updates about your company, upcoming events, or new products. LinkedIn also offers advertising opportunities, which allow you to target specific audiences with ads that appear on LinkedIn's website and in their mobile app.

After you understand the thinking process behind creativity, it becomes easier to increase your creativity. Evaluating too early or too often hinders creative potential. So instead of judging an idea's worthiness right away, try brainstorming lots of ideas first before narrowing them down later.

The following are eight steps that will help you break the bad habit of evaluating too soon and too often:

- Come up with lots of ideas without judgment
- Evaluate the ideas after you have generated a large quantity

- Judge each idea on its own merits
- Consider all possibilities before dismissing any idea
- Don't be afraid to make mistakes—they are part of the creative process
- Be persistent—keep generating new ideas no matter how often you get rejected
- Take time for yourself—relax and let your mind wander
- Be open to change—new perspectives can lead to new insights

Special Tip: PAS Model Problem-Agitate-Solution

The PAS model is a valuable framework for creating new marketing copy ideas. The problem is presented, agitated, and then a solution is proposed. This framework can be used to generate new ideas for ads, blog posts, social media posts, and more.

- Problem: It can be hard to find time to exercise, especially if you have a busy schedule.
- Agitate: Exercising inside can be boring and monotonous. You might not have enough space in your home, or you might not feel comfortable working out in front of other people.
- Solution: Exercise outside! Not only is it more fun and exciting, but you also get to enjoy the fresh air and beautiful scenery. Plus, there are plenty

of outdoor activities that are great for fitness, such as hiking, biking, and running.

- Who doesn't love to exercise? Right….

Paid advertising allows you to target specific audiences with ads that appear on websites and search engine results pages. There are several types of paid advertising, such as Google AdWords, Facebook Ads, and LinkedIn Ads.

Paid advertising can be an effective way to increase traffic to your website but choose the right platform and ad type for your business.

Chapter 7
The Power of Marketing

There once were two small business owners, Sally and John who dreamed of making their business successful. However, they didn't know how to do it. They tried advertising, but that didn't seem to work. They tried changing the product and reinventing it but that didn't seem to work either. One night, they had a revelation. They realized that they needed to market their businesses overnight for them to succeed. And so, they did. Sally and John started by changing the way they marketed their products. They changed their packing label design to include more vibrant colors and attention-grabbing slogans. They also changed their website with almost every form of payment possible (which is key, don't limit to one pay method) and product design to make them more appealing. And it worked! Within a few days, their businesses were thriving and growing. They increased sales and traffic to their businesses almost immediately, and it was all thanks to *Overnight Marketing.* I'm not expecting anything in return for showing you how easy it is to use overnight marketing strategies to improve your business. Unless, of course, you want to reach out and hire me as a coach. But either way, I just want to help businesses grow!

This chapter is the power of marketing. Marketing is a powerful tool that can increase sales and traffic to your business almost immediately. By changing your marketing strategy, you can transform your business almost overnight.

- What is marketing and why is it important
- The different types of marketing and how to use them
- How to create a successful marketing campaign
- The power of SEO and how to use it
- Social media marketing and its benefits
- Offline marketing strategies that still work today
- The future of marketing and how to stay ahead of the curve

For marketing, there are a variety of strategies you can use to be successful. In this chapter, we will discuss some of the most effective marketing strategies and how you can use them to your advantage.

One of the most important aspects of marketing is understanding the different types of marketing. There are many types of marketing, and each is useful in its own way.

Each type of marketing has its own set of benefits and advantages. For example, advertising is great for reaching a large audience quickly and efficiently. Public relations are great for building relationships with customers and clients. SEO is great for increasing traffic to your website.

It's important to understand which type of marketing is best for your business and your goals. If you're not sure which type to use, consult a professional or do some research on your own. Once you have a good understanding of the different types of marketing, you can create a successful marketing campaign.

Creating a successful marketing campaign takes time and effort. But with the right strategy and planning, you can achieve great results. First, you need to come up with a plan that outlines your goals and objectives. Then, you need to create content that aligns with those goals. And lastly, you need to implement a distribution strategy that will reach your target audience.

If you're struggling to come up with a good plan or content ideas, there are plenty of resources online that can help you out. And if you need help implementing a distribution strategy, there are plenty of online tools and services that can help you out as well. There are many resources online that can help you come up with content ideas for your marketing campaign. Some of the best sources of content inspiration include industry publications, blogs, and social media platforms.

Industry publications are a great source of information and inspiration. They offer in-depth insights into what's happening in your industry and can provide ideas for new content topics. Blogs are also a great source of content ideas. They offer a variety of perspectives on current trends and topics, and they can help you find new angles to explore. And lastly, social media platforms are a great source of content inspiration. They offer a variety of content formats, including videos, images, and infographics, and they provide insights into what's popular right now.

The key to success is consistency and patience. If you stick with it and keep improving your campaigns over time, you will see even more success eventually. So don't give up if things don't go as planned; keep trying until you find what works best for your business.

The future of marketing is constantly changing and evolving. To stay ahead of the curve, it's important to stay up to date on the latest trends and changes in the industry. Thankfully, there are plenty of resources available online that can help you do just that. And if you ever get stuck or don't know where to start, don't hesitate to ask for help from professionals or other business owners.

Powerful marketing can differentiate between a successful business and one that fails. Marketing is one of the most important aspects of any business, and if done correctly, it can effectively achieve success. There are many types of marketing, and each has its own set of benefits and advantages. Some of the most common marketing include advertising, public relations, SEO, social media marketing, and offline marketing.

For example, if you want to increase brand awareness, joining civic organizations and getting a promotional tent are excellent places to start. Plus, putting your logo on the tent will help draw people to you. Remember FOMO? Fear Of Missing Out means that people will initially be drawn to your business and want to know more about you. Give your customer what you would want in business, being genuine.

When attempting to increase business, it's crucial that you select a marketing type that will produce the results you desire. If you can't decide on one, speak with someone in the know or read up about the various options. And if by chance you already have a connection who could help... say, maybe the author of this book? Once you have a good understanding of the different types of marketing, you can create a successful marketing campaign.

In summary, let's consider what we learned.

- Start by changing the way you market your products. Make witty and insightful ads that catch people's attention.
- Make changes to your website and product design to make them more appealing.
- Use different types of marketing, such as SEO, social media marketing, and offline marketing strategies (such as radio, handing out flyers, etc.)
- Stay ahead of the curve by learning about the future of marketing and using those techniques in your campaigns. Some examples of staying ahead of the curve in marketing include using chatbots to communicate with customers and using predictive analytics to better understand customer behavior.
- These are just a few of the many techniques that are emerging in the marketing industry. It's important to stay up to date on the latest trends and changes so you can use them in your own campaigns.

Chapter 8

Marketing Your Business on a Budget

When I was just starting out as a small business owner, I was looking to market my business on a budget. I had little money to spend, so I had to be creative. I started by doing some research online, and I found great tips on how to market my business on a budget. When I sold my clients a product, they asked me for help on their social media pages They came to me seeking websites and wanting to know what else they could do next to promote their business. In today's day and age, it is becoming increasingly clear how important having an online presence can be for marketing.

One of the best tips I found was to create a social media profile for my business. I set up a Facebook page and posted updates about my business. I also created a LinkedIn profile for my business and then requested connections with other businesses in my area. I reached out to every company within 50 miles of me, explaining how my business could save them money and increase their sales.

I utilized Google AdWords to advertise my business. I created an ad campaign and targeted people in my area looking for my products or services. Additionally, I added Google Analytics to monitor the efficacy of my ad campaign.

I also used free online tools like Hootsuite and Buffer to help me manage my social media accounts. Hootsuite allowed me to schedule tweets and posts, and Buffer allowed me to queue up posts so they would be released throughout the day. This helped me save time and automate my social media marketing efforts.

By using these affordable marketing methods, I increased traffic to my website and increase sales for my business. My business grew exponentially overnight, and I achieved success without spending a lot of money.

- Understand the basics of marketing your business on a budget
- Use social media to market your business
- Use paid advertising to market your business
- Use free online tools to help you manage your marketing efforts
- Track the results of your marketing efforts
- Celebrate your successes!

Save money and achieve success by understanding how to market your small business on a budget using social media, paid advertising, and free online tools.

To use social media to market your business on a budget, create profiles on popular platforms like Facebook, Twitter, and LinkedIn. Once you have created your profiles, post updates about your products or services. You can also connect with other businesses in your area to create a network. Having a profile for your business on Facebook is less formal than having a page. A profile can be used to connect with friends and family, while a page can be used to connect with customers and clients.

To use paid advertising to market your business on a budget, create an ad campaign using Google AdWords. Target people in your area likely to be interested in your products or services. You can also use Google Analytics to track the results of your ad campaign.

Social Media is essential for small businesses

Customers want to connect with businesses on the platforms they use most, which means having a strong social media presence is more important than ever. There are plenty of benefits to using social media for small businesses. For one, it's a great way to build relationships with customers and create a community around your brand. It's also an efficient way to market your business and reach new customers. Plus, social media can be a great way to get feedback from customers and learn about what they want. With so many benefits, not surprisingly, more small businesses are turning to social media to help them grow.

How to create a social media strategy on a budget

Before you begin allocating a budget for your social media presence, it is important to set some goals. What do you hope to achieve by investing time and energy into social media? Do you want people to become more aware of your brand, or drive traffic toward your website? Knowing what kinds of results you are hoping for will make it easier to measure the success of your strategy down the line. Once you know what you want to achieve, you can plan your content and schedule your posts. It's also important to engage with your audience, so make sure to respond to comments and messages. Finally, don't forget to track your results to see what's working and what's not.

The best social media platforms for small businesses

There are a lot of social media platforms out there, but not all of them are well-suited for small businesses. The best social media platforms for small businesses are where you're likely to find your target audience. For example, if you're targeting millennials, Instagram and Snapchat are good choices. If you're targeting Baby Boomers, Facebook and Twitter are better options. When choosing a platform, it's also important to consider how much time and resources you're willing to invest in it.

How to use paid advertising to market your small business on a budget

Paid advertising is a great way to reach new customers and grow your small business on a budget. The key to success is to create an ad campaign that targets people likely to be interested in your products or services. You can use Google AdWords to create and track your ad campaign. Another option is to use Facebook Ads, which allows you to target people based on their interests and demographics.

Benefits:

- Reach repeat customers
- Grow your business
- Target people likely to be interested in your products or services
- Get your content in front of the right people (word of mouth)
- Increase brand

One shocking fact about paid advertising is that it's possible to lose money if you're not careful. Set realistic goals for your ad campaign and track your results so you can make adjustments as needed. Otherwise, you could spend more money than you're making.

A few other tips with paid advertising

Paid advertising can be overwhelming for small business owners. It doesn't have to be overwhelming, though. You can start small and gradually increase your budget as you get more comfortable with the process.

How to use content marketing to market your small business on a budget

Content marketing is a great way to market your small business on a budget. The key is to create high-quality content that will appeal to your target audience. Once you have some great content, you need to get it in front of the right people. One way to do this is to submit it to directories and blogs that cater to your target audience. Another option is to use social media to share your content and reach new people.

How to track your results and measure success

To ensure your website is running as efficiently as possible, it's key to track your results and analyze what improvements can be made. Google Analytics provides this service for free, so there's no excuse not to take advantage of it! Facebook Insights is another useful tool that provides insights into the reach and engagement of your posts. By tracking your results, you can adjust your strategy as needed to ensure that you get the most out of your marketing efforts.

What type of paid advertising works best for small businesses

For small businesses, paid advertising can be a great way to get noticed. But with so many options available, it's difficult to know where to start. Should you invest in Google ads? Or Facebook ads? Maybe even both? The answer depends on your business and your goals. But there are a few general principles that can help you make the most of paid advertising. First, focus on creating ads that are relevant and targeted to your audience. The more relevant your ad is, the more likely it will be clicked on. Second, make sure your ad stands out from the rest. Use images, video, or other creative elements to grab attention and make your ad memorable. Finally, don't be afraid to experiment. Paid advertising can be a great way to reach new customers and grow your business. But like any marketing strategy, it takes time and effort to get the most out of it. So, start small, track your results, and adjust your approach as you go. With a little trial and error, you'll soon find the paid advertising method that works best for your business.

It depends on a multitude of factors, including the products or services being advertised, the target audience, and the budget. However, some paid advertising methods are more effective than others. Here are a few that are worth considering:

- Pay-per-click (PPC) advertising: PPC ads are a popular form of paid advertising, as they allow businesses to target potential customers actively searching for what they offer.
- Social media advertising: Advertising on social media platforms like Facebook and Instagram can be an effective way to reach small business customers.
- Display advertising: Display ads are another option for small businesses and can be placed on websites and other online platforms.

The best way to determine which paid advertising method will work best for your small business is to experiment with different options and see what produces the best results. Start with a small budget and gradually increase your spending as you see the results. And don't forget to track your progress so you can adjust your strategy as needed.

Paid advertising is a great way to reach new customers, but it's important to remember that it's just one piece of the puzzle. To transform your business overnight, you need to focus on all aspects of your marketing, from your website and social media presence to how you interact with customers. By taking a holistic approach to marketing, you can make dramatic changes that will help you achieve your goals and grow your business.

How to use free online tools to help with marketing

As a business owner, you should always be looking for ways to get an edge on the competition. But you don't have to spend a fortune on marketing consultants or the latest software programs. There are plenty of free online tools that can help you with everything from market research to creating a marketing plan.

One great way to get started is by using Google's Keyword Planner. This tool allows you to see how often particular keywords are being searched for, and it can also help you brainstorm new keyword ideas. You can also use Google Trends to see which topics are getting more popular and consider adding content about those topics to your website. Additionally, Mailchimp offers a free plan that can send out email newsletters. These are a few of the many free online tools that can help with marketing. With so many options available, there is no excuse not to take advantage of these valuable resources. Finally, don't underestimate the power of good old-fashioned networking. Online networking platforms like LinkedIn can be a great way to connect with potential customers and partners. And best of all, it's free! Take advantage of these free online tools to give your business a boost.

How to track the results of your marketing efforts

Marketing is an important tool for any business, but it's difficult to know whether your marketing efforts are paying off. Luckily, there are a few simple ways to track the performance of your marketing campaigns. One way is to analyze the conversion rate of your website. If you see a significant increase in traffic after implementing a new marketing campaign, that's a good sign that your efforts are working. Another way to track your marketing performance is to look at the ROI of your campaigns. This can be done by calculating how much revenue you've generated from each campaign and comparing it to your advertising spend. If you see a positive ROI, that means your campaigns are successful. Finally, don't forget to poll your customers and ask them how they heard about your business. This will give you valuable insights into which marketing channels are most effective for reaching your target audience. By tracking the results of your marketing efforts, you can ensure that you're using your budget effectively.

The importance of customer service

In today's competitive business landscape, it's more important than ever to provide excellent customer service. Your customers are the lifeblood of your business, so you must make them happy. There are a few simple ways to improve your customer service and keep your customers coming back. First, always be polite and professional when dealing with customers. Second, go above and beyond to solve their problems. And third, follow up with them after their purchase to ensure that they're satisfied with your product or service. By providing excellent customer service, you'll build loyalty and repeat business. And that will help you achieve your goals of growing your business overnight.

Tips for celebrating small business success

There's no need to wait for a big milestone to celebrate your small business success. Every day, take a moment to reflect on how far you've come and give yourself a pat on the back. Additionally, celebrate your successes with your team. This will help them feel appreciated and motivated to continue working hard. Finally, don't forget to share your successes with your customers. They'll be happy to hear that you're doing well, and it will solidify their loyalty to your business. So, take time to celebrate your small business success every day, and you'll be well on your way to achieving your goals.

Here are a few facts that even you may be shocked about in terms of customer service:

Eighty-nine percent of consumers are more likely to make another purchase after a positive customer service experience. (Salesforce Research). That's a lot of potential customers that you could be losing if you don't provide good customer service. So, focus on providing excellent customer service and you'll be more likely to keep your customers happy.

Did you know that most businesses don't follow up with their customers after they make a purchase? Following up is key to ensuring customer satisfaction and building loyalty. So, follow up with your customers after they buy from you. It's a simple way to show that you care and are committed to providing excellent customer service.

Nearly three out of five consumers report that good customer service is vital for them to feel loyalty toward a brand. (Zendesk).

Investing in new customers is between 5 and 25 times more expensive than retaining existing ones. (Invesp).

The worst times to call prospects are Mondays and the second half of Fridays. (Callhippo). This can lead to unhappy customers and lost business. The key to building a relationship with your customers is constant communication. Thank them immediately after they've made a purchase, reach out within 24-48 hours of the sale, and then every month or two for 12 months following that initial contact. When we follow up with customers and make friends with them, our retention rates are significantly higher!

With these tips, you can market your small business on a budget and see real results. By setting goals, creating a social media strategy, and using paid advertising, you can reach new customers and grow your business. And don't forget to track your results so you can continue to improve your campaigns. With a little effort, you can see big results from your marketing efforts.

Now that you've read our guide on marketing your small business on a budget, it's time to act. Here are simple steps that you can take to get started:

- Set goals for your marketing efforts. What do you want to achieve? Whether you want to increase sales or drive more traffic to your website, setting measurable goals will help you track your progress and ensure that you're making the most of your marketing budget.

- Create a social media strategy. This is one of the most cost-effective ways to reach new customers and build loyalty with existing ones. Include a mix of content types and target the right channels for your audience.

- Use paid advertising. Paid advertising can be an effective way to reach new customers quickly and efficiently. Target the right people with the right message and you'll see results.

- Track your results. It's important to track the results of your marketing efforts so that you can continue improving them over time. By tracking data such as website visits, conversion rates, and customer feedback, you can make sure that you're using your resources effectively. By following these simple steps, you can market your small business on a budget and seeing real results.

Chapter 9

Finding the Right Customer

It was the early hours of the morning and Tim was exhausted. He had been working tirelessly to increase sales and traffic to his business, but nothing seemed to work. Tim was hopeless. He had tried every marketing strategy imaginable, but nothing seemed to get results. Desperate to find a solution, he turned to Google for help. After browsing through a few articles, he came across a guidebook on how to transform your business overnight by marketing it differently. He was skeptical at first but gave it a try. He quickly implemented the tips in this book and within a few hours, he saw results. Sales were increasing and traffic to his business was growing exponentially. He was amazed at how quickly things had changed and thanked this guidebook for helping him turn his business around. Tim would keep this book in his bag that he brought to work every day as a reminder if he ever had a question about marketing.

This chapter is about finding the right customer. This involves understanding your target market and writing a story that resonates with them. It's also important to be creative and find new ways to reach your target market. By doing this, you can increase sales and traffic to your business almost immediately.

- Who is your target market
- Understand what your customers want
- Write a story that resonates with them'
- Find new ways to reach your target market
- Increase sales and traffic overnight

If you want to find the ideal customer, it is important that you figure out who they are and what they desire. The best way to do this is by conducting research and writing a story that will captivate them. You can also discover new ways to reach your target market through ingenuity and originality.

How to Find the Right Customers for Your Business

With business, one of the most important things you can do is find the right customers. This involves understanding your target market and writing a story that resonates with them.

There are a few steps you can take to find the right customers for your business:

- Do your research—for finding the right customers, you should do research. This means understanding who your target market is and what they want. You can also find new ways to reach your target market by being creative and innovative.

- Write a story that resonates with them—Once you've done your research, it's time to write a story that resonates with your target market. This story should be relatable and offer value to the reader.
- Reach them where they are—It's also important to reach your target market where they are. This means finding new ways to reach them that are creative and innovative.

How to Find the Ideal Customers for Your Business

You can't half-heartedly choose your target market. It's essential that you invest time in understanding them if you want your story to resonate with them. This story should be creative and innovative so you can stand out from your competitors. To reach your target market, you need to be proactive and use various marketing techniques.

Finally, it's important to always be growing and expanding so you can keep up with the ever-changing landscape of business.

How to Understand Your Target Market

You can use various tools, like Google Analytics and social media listening to get a pulse on what people are saying about your industry. Try conducting surveys or interviews so you can get first-hand information from your target demographic. It's also helpful to stay up to date on trends so that you can anticipate changes in the marketplace. This will allow you to cater your products and services to meet the needs of your customers.

Another important part of understanding your target market is knowing where they are located. Knowing this information will help you determine where to allocate your marketing resources. Additionally, you need to understand what motivates your target market. What are their wants and needs? What are they looking for in a product or service? Once you have a good understanding of who your target market is and what they want, you need to create marketing materials that appeal to them. This could include advertisements, website content, or even sales pitches.

It's also important to tailor your sales process to match the needs of your target market. If they're not comfortable with purchasing large online, then make sure you have a physical location where they can purchase your products or services. Finally, remember that it takes time and effort to properly understand your target market. Don't expect to get it right the first time around; continue doing research and adjusting your strategy until you find what works best for you and your business.

For example, Vinyl flooring companies often try to be the cheapest. Furthermore, we can go on social media pages and groups for this product to get a wider variety of customer feedback instead of just relying on review sites. This way, we can provide better customer service and win over more potential buyers!

How to Write a Story That Resonates with Your Target Market

Now that you know who your target market is and what they want, it's time to write a story that resonates with them. This story should be creative, innovative and offer value to the reader. It should be something that they can relate to and that will make them want to do business with you. Remember, your goal is to stand out from your competition, so don't be afraid to be different. Use your unique voice and perspective to tell a story no one else can tell. For writing content that resonates with your target market, it's important to understand your brand voice and identity. Once you know who you are as a brand, it will be much easier to produce content that resonates with your target market. This content should be original, useful, and engaging.

The goal is to create a connection with your audience, so they keep coming back for more. To do this, you need to understand what your target market is interested in. Once you know who your target market is and what they're interested in, you need to create content that speaks to them. This could be anything from blog posts to social media updates. The key is to make sure that the content you produce is high quality and relevant to your audience. If you can do that, then you'll be well on your way to creating connections that will help your business grow.

When writing your story, remember these tips:

- Start with a strong hook—The first few sentences of your story are vital in grabbing the reader's attention. Have a strong opening that will make them want to continue reading.
- Write in a relatable way—Use language and examples that your target market can relate to. This will help them connect with your story on a personal level.

- Be clear and concise—Don't cram too much information into your story. Keep it short and sweet so the reader can easily digest it.

- Use emotion—Emotion is a powerful tool that can influence the reader's decision-making process. Appeal to their emotions to get them to act.

- Offer value—What can the reader gain from reading your story? Offer value to keep them engaged.

- Be unique—it's important to differ from your competition. Use your uniqueness to your advantage and write a story that will make you stand out.

- Edit and revise—Don't publish your story without first editing and revising it. This will help ensure that it is error-free and flows well.

People want to do business with people they can relate to. So many businesses talk about themselves but don't add any value. If you're passionate, show it through your branding and social media posts; what is the vision or mission for your company in this world?

How to Be Creative and Reach Your Target Market

There are countless ways to reach your target market these days. It's no longer enough to rely on traditional marketing techniques like print ads or TV commercials. Instead, you need to get creative and think outside the box.

- Influencer marketing—This involves working with popular individuals or brands in your industry to promote your products or services. This can be done through sponsored posts, social media takeovers, or even product placement.

- Guerilla marketing—This is a type of unconventional marketing that relies on shock value and creativity to get attention. It's often used for small businesses that don't have the budget for traditional marketing techniques.

- Targeted ads—These are ads that are specifically targeted at people who are interested in what you have to offer. This could be done through social media, search engines, or even retargeting ads.

- Public relations—This involves generating positive press coverage for your business through media outreach and press releases.

- Event marketing—This is a great way to get people talking about your business by hosting or sponsoring events.

- Content marketing—This involves creating and distributing high-quality content relevant to your target market. This could be anything from blog posts to infographics to videos.

The important thing is to remember that you need to be creative to reach your target market. With so many options available, there's no excuse not to try something new. So get out there and experiment until you find what works best for your business.

For finding the right customers for your business, you should take the time to understand who your target market is. This means doing research and learning everything you can about them. You can also find new ways to reach your target market by being creative and innovative.

After you identify your target market, it's time to start writing content that interests them. Your content should be unique, useful, and engaging so that you form a connection with your readers and listeners. Ideally, they will keep coming back for more of your original work. To produce content aligned with your brand identity, you first need to clearly understand who you are as a brand. Once you have established that, creating resonating content will be much simpler.

It's essential to use various marketing techniques to reach your target market. Consider using influencer marketing or guerilla marketing tactics so you can reach people where they are already spending their time. Try using targeted ads on social media or search engines so you can specifically reach people interested in what you offer. The sky's the limit with creativity, so don't be afraid to experiment until you find what works best for your business.

One way to be creative and reach your target market is to use shock value in your marketing efforts. This could involve using outrageous ads or stunts that get people's attention. It's important to stand out from the competition and using something very informative or funny is a great way to do that. So, get creative with your marketing and see what results you can achieve.

Now that you understand the basics of how to reach your target market, it's time to put it into practice. This means being creative and using various marketing techniques to get your message out there. It also means understanding who your target market is and writing content that speaks to them. Finally, be proactive and use various marketing techniques to reach your target market. Finding the right customers is essential for any business owner or marketing professional. By understanding your target market and writing a story that resonates with them, you can increase sales and traffic almost immediately. Get creative and try new things so you can stand out from your competition. Constantly grow and expand so you can stay up to date with changing trends.

Chapter 10
Online Marketing Techniques That Work

When I was starting out in business, I was looking for ways to market my company online. I quickly realized that there were a lot of different techniques that could be used, and it initially felt quite overwhelming. After trying out a few different methods and seeing which ones worked best for me, I narrowed it down to three techniques that have always worked well for my company.

The first technique is called social media marketing. This involves creating profiles for your company on various social media platforms, such as Facebook, Twitter, and LinkedIn. You can then post updates and links to your website on these profiles, which will help to increase traffic to your site. The great thing about social media marketing is that it's free to do, and it can be a great way to connect with your customers.

The second technique is search engine optimization, or SEO. This involves optimizing your website, so it appears higher in the search results when people search for keywords related to your business. By doing this, you'll get more visitors to your website, which can lead to more sales. There are a lot of things you can do to optimize your website, such as adding keywords to your titles and descriptions, and optimizing your images.

The third technique is email marketing. This involves listing email addresses of people interested in what you offer, and then sending them regular emails containing information about your products or services. You can also include links to your website or special offers in these emails, which can help to increase traffic and sales.

These online marketing techniques can be a great way to promote your business and help it grow. Try out a few and see which ones work best for you.

Online marketing techniques can be a great way to promote your business and help it grow.

Introduce social media marketing

Social media marketing is the process of creating profiles on online platforms like Facebook, Twitter, and LinkedIn to generate interest in your company and its products or services. By posting updates regularly, you can encourage potential customers to visit your website more often.

One of the great things about social media marketing is that it provides businesses with a way to connect with their customers in a personal way. By creating and managing social media accounts, businesses can communicate with their customers directly, answer questions, and provide support. This helps to create a connection between the customer and the business, which can lead to increased loyalty and sales. Additionally, social media platforms are a great way to share news and up-dates about your business, which can help to keep customers informed and interested. The best way to grow your following is by constantly posting high-quality content. Your posts will keep people interested in what you have going on, and before long they'll be the ones boosting YOUR business!

Introducing SEO

Search engine optimization, or SEO, is optimizing your website so it appears higher in the search results when people search for keywords related to your business. This can be done by adding keywords to your titles and descriptions and optimizing your images. By doing this, you'll get more visitors to your website, which can lead to more sales.

What does SEO do for websites? When people search for keywords related to your business on a search engine such as Google, the results that appear are determined by several factors, one of which is the position of your website in the search results. The higher up your website appears, the more likely it is that people will click on it. By optimizing your website for SEO, you can improve your chances of appearing higher in the search results, which will lead to more traffic and potential customers.

How can SEO help you get more visitors to your website

Did you know that by simply optimizing your website for the search engines, you have a greater chance of appearing higher in the results when people enter keywords related to your business? In other words, more customers will be able to find you. By optimizing your website images and adding relevant keywords to your titles and descriptions, you will not only improve traffic but also increase the chances of potential customers finding your site when they search for information related to your products or services.

The benefits of SEO reach beyond simple increases in website traffic. It also helps you cultivate relationships with customers and earn their trust, in addition to boosting your brand's authority. By following these tips, you can improve your website's SEO and attract more visitors.

There are several things you can do to improve your website's SEO, including:

Optimize your title tags and meta descriptions

- Your title tags and meta descriptions are important elements of your website's SEO, so include relevant keywords and phrases. This will help your website show up in search results for those keywords.

- Use keyword-rich content. To improve your website's SEO, you must use keyword-rich content throughout your site. This includes using keywords in page titles, headings, and body text. Try to use synonyms and related keywords to diversify your keyword usage.

Optimize your images

- In addition to using keywords in your text, you can also optimize your images by including relevant keywords in the file names and alt text. This will help your images show up in search results for those keywords.

Create quality backlinks

- Backlinks are when other websites link to yours, and they play a crucial role in how well your website ranks on search engines. To improve your website's SEO, you must create quality backlinks from high-quality websites. You can do this by guest blogging, creating informative blog posts, or adding your website to directories and listings.

Introduce email marketing

- Email marketing is the process of creating and sending newsletters, special offers, and other promotional materials to a list of customers or subscribers. This can be an effective way to increase traffic to your website and generate sales. Additionally, email marketing can build relationships with customers and keep them informed about your business.

What and how can email marketing help you in the new digital era?

Email marketing has been around for over 30 years. You can use retargeting emails to potential and previous buyers after sending out a mass email. This increases the likelihood of customers converting into sales. It can also help you build relationships with customers, as well as engage them in conversations about your product or service.

- Email marketing is a great way to increase traffic to your website and generate sales. By sending newsletters, special offers, and other promotional materials to a list of customers or subscribers, you'll be able to interest more people in your business. Additionally, email marketing can build relationships with customers and keep them informed about your business. This can lead to increased loyalty and sales.

  Email marketing is an effective way to stay top-of-mind for potential customers who may not have been ready to purchase yet. Lastly, it's a low cost and effective way to reach a large audience with minimal effort.

- When creating a social media profile for your company, it's important to consider what information you want to include and how you want to present it. You'll also need to decide which social media platform(s) you want to use. Once you've done this, you can create your profile and share content with your followers. Additionally, interact with other users and respond to comments and questions to build relationships with potential customers.

  First, what information do you want to include? How do you want to present it? It's important to put your best foot forward, but you also don't want to overshare. Once you've got that figured out, you must decide which social media platform(s) you want to use. Will Twitter be your jam? Or are you more of a LinkedIn aficionado? Once you've created your profile, it's time to share content with your followers. But don't stop there! Interact with other users and respond to comments and questions. This is a great way to build relationships with potential customers. So go forth and socialize!

Tips for posting updates on social media profiles

When creating content for your social media profile, it's important to consider what your followers will find interesting or valuable. Also, try to post regularly to keep your followers engaged. Additionally, interact with other users and respond to comments and questions to build relationships with potential customers. Try sharing links to articles, images, or other content that your followers will find useful or entertaining. You can also post about upcoming events, new products or services, or promotions. By keeping these things in mind, you can create updates that will help you connect with your followers and promote your business.

With social media, it's important to keep your followers engaged by posting updates regularly. However, simply posting anything and everything can have the opposite effect.

Here are a few tips for posting updates that will keep your followers interested:

- Your followers will appreciate posts that are valuable and interesting, so provide content that is worth their time. This could include news articles, blog posts, or even interesting facts or quotes.

- Post regularly, but not too often. It's important to post regularly, but you don't want to bombard your followers with too many updates. Try to space out your posts so your followers have something new to look forward to each time they check your profile.

Interact with other users. Social media is all about interaction, so respond to comments and questions from other users. This will help you build relationships with potential customers. Finally, don't forget to have fun!

Blogging and its benefits

Blogging is a great way to connect with potential customers and promote your business. By sharing valuable and interesting content, you can attract new readers to your blog and build relationships with them. Blogging is a great way to share information about your business and build relationships with potential customers. By writing informative and engaging blog posts, you'll be able to attract more people to your website and generate interest in your products or services. Blogging can help you improve your search engine ranking, which can lead to more traffic to your website. Additionally, by responding to comments and questions, you'll be able to create a dialogue with your readers and build rapport. So why not try it?

Tips for writing effective blog posts

- When writing a blog post, you must consider your audience and what they'll find interesting or valuable. Also try to make your posts engaging and easy to read.

- Your readers will appreciate posts that are well-written and informative, so provide valuable content. This could include news articles, blog posts, or even interesting facts or quotes. Also break up your text with headings and sub-headings to help organize your thoughts.

Keep your posts short and sweet. Most readers won't want to read a long, drawn-out post, so try to keep your posts short and sweet. You can always save the details for another post.

Be interactive with your readers

- Social media is all about interaction, so respond to comments and questions from other users. This will help you build relationships with potential customers.

- When writing a blog post, it's important to consider what your readers will find interesting or valuable. Also, try to keep your posts informative and engaging. Respond to comments and questions to create a dialogue with your readers and build a rapport. Now that you know how to write an effective blog post, it's time to put your skills to work. Try writing a few posts and see what happens. The results may surprise you. Additionally, don't forget to use social media to share your content with a wider audience. By following these tips, you'll be able to create interesting and engaging blog posts that will help promote your business.

Introduce the concept of PPC and its benefits

PPC is short for pay-per-click, a type of online advertising that allows you to pay for placement in search engine results pages. This is a great way to attract more visitors to your site, generate more leads, or make more sales. Additionally, PPC can help you build trust with potential customers and establish your brand as an authority in your industry.

Offer tips for successful PPC campaigns

There are several things you can do to create a successful PPC campaign, including:

- Researching keywords that relate to your business or the market you are trying to enter is essential.
- Before you create your ad, use Google AdWords Keyword Planner to research relevant keywords for your business. Doing so will increase the effectiveness of your ad. After you've hand-picked the most relevant keywords for your campaign, be sure to work them into your ad copy.

Create compelling ad copy

Your advertising should be easy to understand, direct, and convincing. End with a strong call to action so those interested can easily find out more about your product or service. Use relevant images. In addition to your ad copy, you'll also want to use relevant images in your ads. Use images that are easy to understand and support your text.

Target your audience

When creating your PPC campaign, target your audience with relevant keywords and ad copy. You can also use targeting options like location and demographics to ensure that your ads are shown to the people most likely to convert.

Retargeting and its benefits

Retargeting is online advertising that allows you to show ads to people who have visited your website. This is a great way to remind potential customers about your product or service, and it can help increase brand awareness and generate more leads or sales.

Tips for successful retargeting campaigns

There are several things you can do to create a successful retargeting campaign, including:

- Install the Facebook pixel on your website.
- The Facebook pixel is a code that allows you to track visitors to your website. Once you've installed the pixel, you can create targeted ads

that will be shown to people who have visited your site.

Use relevant images

In addition to your ad copy, you'll also want to use relevant images in your ads. These images should be clear and concise, and they should help convey your message.

A/B testing and its benefits

A/B testing is a type of online experimentation that allows you to test two versions of an ad or landing page against each other. This is a great way to see which version performs better and make more informed decisions about your online marketing.

Tips for successful A/B tests

There are several things you can do to create a successful A/B test, including:

Choose your objective

- Before you start your A/B test, you must choose the objective you want to test. This could be something like click-through rate, conversion rate, or time on page.

Select your metric

- Once you've chosen your objective, you must select the metric you want to use to measure success. This could be something like number of clicks, conversion rate, or time on page.

Create your variants

- After you've selected your objective and metric, you must create the two variants you want to test. These could be different versions of an ad or landing page.

Run your test

- Once you've created your variants, you must run your test and collect data. You can use tools like Google Analytics to track the performance of each variant.

Analyze your results

- After you've collected data from your A/B test, you must analyze the results to see which variant performed better. You can use tools like Google Analytics to help you with this.

There are several things you can do to increase your online sales and traffic overnight, including:

- Use relevant images.
- Target your audience.
- Use retargeting campaigns.
- A/B test your ads and landing pages.
- Analyze your results and make changes.

By following these tips, you can make your business more successful almost immediately. Implementing these changes will help you increase sales and traffic, and it will also help you build a more successful business overall.

Special Tip: AIDA Marketing

- AIDA marketing is a model that helps you create effective marketing campaigns by focusing on the needs of your customers. The model consists of four steps: attention, interest, desire, and action.

- You should focus on getting your customers' attention, arousing their interest, convincing them to want your product or service, and then motivating them to take action. You can use the AIDA marketing technique to create ads that are more likely to capture attention, interest, desire, and action from your target audience.

- Attention: Do you love cookies?

- Interest: Who doesn't love cookies? They're delicious, sweet, and perfect for satisfying your cravings.

- Desire: Imagine being able to enjoy fresh, warm cookies right out of the oven whenever you want. With "Overnight's" cookie delivery service, that's exactly what you can do. We'll deliver fresh cookies right to your doorstep.

- Action: Order "Overnight's" cookie delivery service today!

- See what I did there? Replace "Overnight" with your business and rinse and repeat!

Chapter 11

How To Get Your Business out into the Community

One of the best ways to get your business out into the community is by participating in local events. This can include things like fairs, festivals, and farmers' markets. Participation in local events allows you to contact potential customers and promote your business. It also gives people a chance to learn more about what you do and how you can help them.

If you're looking for a way to transform your business almost immediately, then participating in local events is a great place to start.

Here are tips on how to get the most out of this marketing strategy:

Do your research. Not all local events are created equal. Some may be more relevant to your target market than others. When you're doing your research, keep your target market in mind. This will help you choose the right events to participate in.

Get involved early. Many local events have Vendor Applications that need to be filled out and submitted well in advance. If you wait until the last minute, you may not get a spot at the event.

Promote, promote, promote. Once you've secured a spot at a local event, it's important to promote it. Let your current customers know that you'll be attending. You can also promote it through social media and other online channels.

Make it a team effort. If you have employees, enlist their help in manning your booth or table at the event. This will free you to talk to potential customers and answer any questions they may have.

Follow up with leads. After the event is over, follow up with any leads you received. This is an important step in converting them into paying customers. When participating in a local event, it's important to make the most of the opportunity.

Have a plan

If you're like me, you probably don't plan far in advance. You might plan your weekend a few days ahead of time, or maybe you plan your vacation a few weeks in advance. But with bigger events, such as a trade show or conferences, many people don't plan. This is a huge mistake! Having a plan before you go to an event will help you make the most of your time there. There's nothing worse than showing up to an event unprepared. Whether it's a networking mixer or a friend's birthday party, arriving without a plan can often lead to wasted time and opportunity. That's why it's always a good idea to have a plan in place before you go. By taking a few minutes to think about your goals for the event, you'll be better able to make the most of your time there. And who knows, with a little planning, you might just be the life of the party.

Figure out your goals for the event

What do you hope to accomplish? Do you want to meet new people, learn about new products, or find new suppliers? Once you know your goals, you can create a plan to achieve them.

Make a list of the people you want to meet. This might include potential customers, suppliers, or other industry experts. If you have a specific person in mind, do some research ahead of time so you can make the most of your conversation.

Familiarize yourself with the event schedule and map out which sessions or activities you want to attend. This will help you make the most of your time and ensure that you miss nothing important.

Pack light

Bring only the essentials so you can move around easily and talk to people without being encumbered by bags or luggage.

Bring samples or brochures

One of the most important things to remember when exhibiting at a trade show is to bring samples or brochures to potential customers. This will allow them to learn more about what you do and how you can help them. You don't want to be too pushy—no one likes a hard sell—but a little information can go a long way in helping people make an informed decision about your product or service. So, next time you're exhibiting, bring plenty of samples and brochures! You never know when you'll make a sale. Plus, it'll show that you're a professional, serious about their business.

Dress for success

When exhibiting at a trade show, first impressions are key. You want potential customers to see your booth or table and instantly be impressed. How do you achieve this? By dressing for success! Make sure you and your team are wearing professional attire that makes you look put-together and trustworthy. In addition, be sure your signage is legible and that everything is neatly arranged. A little effort goes a long way in making a good impression on potential customers. So, dress for success and watch your business thrive.

Be prepared to talk to people

When people stop by your booth, be prepared to talk to them. The more information you can provide, the better. If you're selling a product, the #1 rule is to be prepared to talk to people. When people stop by your booth, they'll want to know all about what you're selling. The more information you can provide, the better. In addition to talking about your product, be sure to Smile! People are more likely to buy from someone they like, so it's important to make a good impression. And finally, don't forget to close the sale. If you've done your job right, the customer will be interested in buying your product. But you must ask for the sale to seal the deal. Follow these tips, and you'll be sure to talk to people like a pro in no time! Customers are more likely to visit businesses run by people who seem happy and amicable, so remember to smile and be prepared to answer any questions they might have.

Follow up after the event

You cannot stop marketing yourself even when the event is over. You must keep working towards your goal. Send a thank-you note or email to everyone you met and include any information or brochures they might find helpful. This will help keep your name top-of-mind and show that you're a professional serious about growing their business. Plus, it's just good manners!

Follow up with leads

Congratulations, you did it! You survived the event and collected a bunch of leads. Now the hard part begins, following up. This is an essential step in converting leads into paying customers, but it can also be daunting. After the event is over, follow up with any leads you received. The best way to do this is to send a personal email or call them within 24 hours of receiving their information. You can thank them for coming to the event and express your interest in working with them further. This will help you build a relationship and establish trust. If you don't follow up, you're likely to lose their business to someone who does. So, stay in touch and turn those leads into loyal customers.

You don't want to seem needy or pushy

Here are a few tips to help you navigate the follow-up process:

- First, decide how you will follow up. Will you call, email, or both?

- Next, make a plan. What are you going to say? Keep it short and sweet.

- Finally, act! Follow up with your leads as soon as possible. The sooner you reach out, the better.

Implement what you've learned

Now that you know how to market your business overnight, it's time to put what you've learned into action. Make some changes and see how they impact your business. You might be surprised at how quickly things can change when you market your business the right way. So, wait no longer, get started today and see the transformation for yourself. Good luck!

Implementing what you've learned is essential for seeing results

Remember that it takes time to see results from any marketing campaign—so don't give up overnight. You might be surprised at how quickly things can change when you make some changes and see how they impact your business. If you're not sure where to start, why not try implementing a few of these tips:

- Reach your customers on social media and ask for their feedback.

- Make it easy for customers to leave reviews on your website or popular review sites.

- Host an event or promotion and offer discounts to customers who attend.

- Write blog posts or articles about topics that your customers are interested in.

Implementing even a few of these tips can make a world of difference for your business.

Keep learning

Marketing is an ever-changing field, so it's important to keep learning and growing. There are always new strategies and tactics to learn, so stay up to date on the latest trends. The more you know, the better equipped you'll be to market your business successful. There are a few easy ways to stay informed about the latest marketing trends:

- Read marketing blogs or articles.
- Follow marketing experts on social media.
- Attend marketing events or conferences.
- Join a marketing organization or networking group.

No matter how you stay informed, make sure you're always learning and growing as a marketer or business. The more you know, the better equipped you'll be to take your business to the next level.

By following these simple tips, you can create a plan to help you make the most of your time at any event. So next time an event is coming up, don't wait until the last minute to plan— focus on these key points and you'll have a successful event experience. You'll be sure to have a successful event and turn those leads into customers. So, get out there and grow your business!

Did you know that only 2% of leads are followed up? (unknown). That means that 98% of leads are lost forever - a huge, missed opportunity. So, follow up with any leads you receive and do it as soon as possible. The sooner you reach out, the better.

The best way to market your business overnight is by using tried and true methods that have succeeded for other businesses. However, there are always new strategies and tactics to learn.

Now that you know how to market your business overnight, it's time to put what you've learned into action. Make some changes and see how they impact your business. You might be surprised at how quickly things can change when you market your business correctly. Wait no longer, get started today and see the transformation for yourself. Good luck! Here are a few other tips to help remind you:

- Implementing what you've learned is essential for seeing results. Remember that it takes time to see results from any marketing campaign—so don't give up overnight.

- Reach your customers on social media and ask for their feedback.

- Make it easy for customers to leave reviews on your website or popular review sites.

- Host an event or promotion and offer discounts to customers who attend.

- Write blog posts or articles about topics that your customers are interested in.

- Keep learning. There are always new strategies and tactics to learn and stay up to date on the latest trends. The more you know, the better equipped you'll be to market your business successfully.

- Follow up with any leads you receive and do it as soon as possible. The sooner you reach out, the better.

- Use tried and true methods that have succeeded for other businesses, but always be on the lookout for new strategies to try.

If you follow these pointers, you'll optimize your time spent at local events and better your chances of success. With that being said, have a prosperous event and turn prospects into regulars! Get out there to expand your enterprise!

Chapter 12

Business Ethics and Why They Matter More Than Ever

The business world is a tricky place. To be successful, you need to be assertive and competitive. However, if you want people in your field to respect you, it's important that you maintain a high level of ethics and integrity.

Recently, there have been several high-profile cases of businesses cutting corners and engaging in unethical behavior. This has led to a lot of public backlashes and has caused people to lose trust in businesses.

As a business owner, it's important to remember that your customers are the most important thing you have. If you lose their trust, you'll lose everything. Always act with integrity and honesty, and never compromise your values for profit. Your customers will thank you for it.

- What is business ethics and why do they matter
- The importance of business honesty and integrity

- How to act with integrity in difficult situations
  The consequences of unethical behavior
- Tips for maintaining a high level of ethics in your business

In the business world, ethics and integrity are key. If you cut corners and act unethically, you will lose the trust of your customers, which can be damaging to your business.

Maintaining a high level of ethics is not always easy, but it is important. Make sure that your values never take a backseat to profits. Be honest with your customers at all times. Don't engage in any dishonest or unethical behavior. Remember that your customers are the most important thing you have.

The Importance of Honesty and Integrity in Business

Honesty and integrity are essential in the business world. If you are dishonest with your customers, they will not trust you or your business. This can lead to lost sales and can damage your reputation. It is important to always be honest with your customers. This means being open about your products and services and being truthful in your marketing and advertising. Also, avoid engaging in any unethical or illegal behavior. If you act with honesty and integrity, you will maintain the trust of your customers and build a strong reputation for your business. Business ethics are important for several reasons. First, they help to ensure that businesses are operating in a fair and transparent way.

This helps to create trust between businesses and their customers, which is essential for long-term success. Second, business ethics help to promote a positive corporate culture.

This can be beneficial for both employees and customers, as it creates an environment that is respectful and collaborative. Finally, business ethics help to protect the reputation of both businesses and the business community. This is important because it helps to ensure that the business community is viewed positively by the public, which can help to attract new customers and business partners. Ultimately, business ethics are important for both businesses and the business community.

The Consequences of Unethical Behavior

There's no doubt that business ethics are important. No one wants to be associated with a company that engages in unethical behavior. But what are the consequences of unethical behavior? Well, they can be severe. Unethical behavior can damage a company's reputation. If word gets out that a company is engaging in shady business practices, it can be difficult to win back the trust of consumers and business partners. Furthermore, unethical practices can often lead to legal trouble. If a company is caught violating laws or regulations, it could face hefty fines or even jail time for its executives.

Additionally, unethical behavior can lead to a loss of trust from your customers. If they no longer trust you or your business, they will take their business elsewhere. This can have a devastating impact on your bottom line. Finally, unethical behavior can damage the business community. When businesses engage in dishonest or illegal practices, it makes the business community look bad. This can make it difficult for other businesses to succeed.

So, as you can see, ethical behavior is important for both businesses and the business community. If you want your business to succeed, you need to make sure you are always behaving in an ethical manner.

Tips for Maintaining a High Level of Ethics in Your Business

There are a few things you can do to help ensure that your business always acts with integrity and ethics:

- Meanwhile, check that your principles are in line with what you do. For example, if maintaining a good reputation is something you say is important to you, be sure that this quality controls everything you do. Be transparent in your dealings with customers. They should always know what they are getting from you, and never try to hide anything from them.

- Avoid any illegal or unethical behavior. This will only harm your business in the long run.

- One of the most shocking things about business ethics is that many companies still engage in unethical behavior, despite the severe consequences. This can be because they believe that the benefits of breaking the law or engaging in dishonest practices outweigh the risks. Unfortunately, this often leads to even bigger problems later. So, while it may seem like a good idea engaging in unethical behavior, is always a bad choice for businesses.

- Treat your employees fairly and with respect. They are an essential part of your business, and they deserve to be treated well.

- Make sure that you are always learning. The business world is constantly changing, and you need to make sure that you are keeping up with the latest developments.

- If you follow these tips, you can maintain a high level of ethics in your business. This is important because it will help you keep the trust of your customers and will ensure that your business is successful. Also, this helps maintain a good reputation, attract new customers, and ensure long-term success.

- Now that you understand the importance of business ethics and why it's so important to behave ethically, it's time to consider some specific tips for maintaining a high level of ethics in your own business. Here are a few things you can do:

- Creating customer loyalty starts with having shared values. When your company's values are in line with your customers, they're more likely to trust you and be open to a positive relationship if any issues arise.

- Be transparent in your dealings with customers. They should always know what they are getting from you, and never try to hide anything from them. Avoid any illegal or unethical behavior. This will only harm your business eventually.

- Treat your employees fairly and with respect. They are an essential part of your business, and they deserve to be treated well. Finally, make sure that you are always learning.

Chapter 13

Telling Your Story

One of the best ways to market your business is by telling your story. Your story is what makes you unique, and it can be a powerful tool to connect with customers and create loyalty. When you tell your story, focus on the human elements, the emotions and experiences that your customers can relate to. Share your story in a way that is genuine and authentic, and make sure that it is consistently reflected in your branding and marketing efforts.

For example, if you own a pet store, you could tell the story of how you got into the business and why you are passionate about animals. You could share stories of customers who have found the perfect pet for their family, or of employees who have gone above and beyond to help care for the animals. These stories will help customers connect with your brand and see you as more than a store. They'll see you as a trusted source of information and a caring business owner.

Some key points to remember when telling your story: focus on the human elements, be genuine and authentic, and make sure your story is reflected in your branding. Telling your story is a great way to connect with customers and create loyalty.

- Storytelling
- Why storytelling is important for businesses
- How to tell your story effectively
- Tips for crafting a powerful story
- Examples of businesses that use storytelling well

Storytelling

Storytelling has been used for centuries to entertain, educate and inspire people. It's a powerful tool for businesses as well. It can help you build trust with your customers, create meaningful connections and make your business stand out from the competition. In this chapter, we'll discuss why storytelling is important for businesses and how you can use it to your advantage.

Why Storytelling is Important for Businesses

Telling your story can help strengthen your brand, engage customers and drive conversions. It's also a great way to showcase your values and differentiate yourself from other businesses in the same industry. Storytelling helps businesses engage their customers in a meaningful way. It allows them to share the values, mission, and goals of the business in a relatable way that resonates with customers.

How to Tell Your Story Effectively

Your story is a crucial aspect of your business that should be honest and based on your true identity. It's also necessary for it to go hand-in-hand with the image you've presented in your branding and marketing campaign.

Tips for Crafting a Powerful Story

Figure out why you first decided to start your company. Oftentimes, we keep that part of our journey hidden because we're ashamed of where we began or how poor we were. It's easy to believe that people won't want to work with us if they knew how hard we've worked and all the challenges we faced to get where we are. However, this could be the key to connecting with your customers. Share stories about how you overcame obstacles to succeed. This can help build trust and loyalty with potential customers, making them more likely to purchase from you or recommend your business to others.

Examples of Businesses that use Storytelling Well

You don't have to look far for examples of businesses that use storytelling effectively. Many successful companies, such as Apple and Starbucks, have created powerful stories around their products and services. As you look at these examples, think about how they tell their stories in a way that resonates with customers and creates loyalty. Many smaller businesses have found success through storytelling, such as pet stores that share stories about their animals and the people who go beyond to help care for them. These stories will help customers connect with your brand and see you as more than a store.

They'll see you as a trusted source of information and a caring business owner. Whatever type of business you are, storytelling can be an effective way to engage customers. Storytelling is a key ingredient for success, no matter how large or small your business may be. By taking the time to craft a powerful story, you can create meaningful connections with your customers and establish yourself as a trusted source.

Keep these things mind while you're telling your story:

- Make sure your story is focused on the human element. Share the emotions and experiences that your customers can relate to.

- Be genuine and authentic in your storytelling. Your story should reflect your brand and who you are as a business.

- Use concrete examples and stories to illustrate your points. Share stories to customers or employees that illustrate the human element of your business.

- Keep your story short. You don't need to share every detail of your business history, just focus on the key points that will connect with customers and make them want to learn more.

- Keep your story focused on the positive aspects of your business. You want to share experiences and emotions that will create a positive association with your brand.

By following these tips, you can create a powerful story that connects with customers and builds loyalty for your business

Now that you understand the importance of storytelling for businesses, it's time to put these tips into practice. Start by introducing your story to customers in a way that is genuine and authentic. Make sure your story is reflected in your branding and marketing materials.

Practice telling your story regularly, and ensure it always focuses on the positive aspects of your business. By following these tips, you can create a powerful story that connects with customers and builds loyalty for your brand.

Chapter 14
Creating a Unique Selling Proposition

To stand out in today's competitive market, it's important to have a unique selling proposition (USP). Your USP makes you different from your competitors, and it should be reflected in everything from your branding to your marketing efforts. When creating your USP, focus on what perhaps nobody else can. This could be anything from a unique product or service to an exceptional customer experience. Once you've identified your USP, communicate it clearly to potential customers.

- What is a Unique Selling Proposition (USP)?
- How do you identify your USP?
- Why is having a USP important for businesses today?
- How can you communicate your USP to potential customers effectively?
- Examples of successful businesses with strong USPs

What is a Unique Selling Proposition (USP)?

A USP is a key component of any successful business. It is what makes you different from your competitors, and it should be reflected in everything from your branding to your marketing efforts.

How do you identify your USP?

The first step in creating a USP is identifying what makes you unique. This could be anything from a unique product or service to an exceptional customer experience. Once you've identified your USP, communicate it clearly to potential customers.

Why is having a USP important for businesses today?

In today's competitive market, it's important to have a USP that sets you apart from your competitors. With a strong USP, you can attract more customers and increase sales. When potential customers are looking for a product or service, you want them to think of your business first.

How can you communicate your USP to potential customers effectively?

Once you've identified your USP, you need to communicate it effectively to potential customers. This can be done in various ways, such as through your branding, website, marketing materials, and sales pitches. There are many other ways to communicate your USP to potential customers. Some effective methods also include marketing collateral such as brochures and flyers, as well as online tools such as website banner ads and social media posts.

Examples of successful businesses with strong USPs

To be successful in business, it's important to have a unique selling proposition (USP). This makes you different from your competitors, and it should be reflected in everything from your branding to your marketing efforts. When creating your USP, focus on what perhaps nobody else can. This could be anything from a unique product or service to an exceptional customer experience.

There are numerous examples of successful businesses with strong USPs. Some notable examples include Apple, Amazon, and Southwest Airlines. Each company has a unique selling proposition that differentiates them from its competitors. To do this, you must focus on what makes you stand out and articulate it in a way that is clear and memorable. You'll also need to ensure that your USP is reflected in all aspects of your marketing efforts. By doing these things, you can set yourself apart from the competition and increase sales and traffic to your business.

Remember: focus on what makes you different from your competitors, communicate it clearly to potential customers, and ensure it is reflected in your branding and marketing efforts. Having a unique selling proposition is a great way to stand out in today's competitive market.

Chapter 15

Should You Use a Funnel for Marketing?

Funnel marketing is a great way to increase sales and traffic to your business. A funnel is a process you use to convert leads into customers. It's a great way to target your audience and get them interested in what you offer. There are several steps to using a funnel, and it's important to follow each step to succeed.

However, before we dive too deep into funnel marketing, let's first discuss lead magnets. Lead magnets are an effective means of gaining the attention of potential customers and ultimately converting them into leads. The lead magnet or offer should be something highly valuable to your target audience so that you can funnel more prospects later. Examples of lead magnets include free e-books, checklists, and webinars.

There are several steps to creating a lead magnet:

- Identify the problem your lead magnet will solve.
- Determine the audience you want to reach with your lead magnet.

- Identify the content you will include in your lead magnet.

- Create a catchy headline for your lead magnet.

- Design a compelling cover for your lead magnet.

- Write an attention-grabbing introduction to your lead magnet.

- Write clear and concise instructions for how to use your lead magnet.

- Include testimonials from happy customers who have used your lead magnet.

- Promote your lead magnet on social media and other online platforms.

- Follow up with leads who download your lead magnet to ensure they are using it correctly and getting the results they want.

For example, our "Ultimate Guide to Vehicles" would be a great lead magnet for anyone wanting to learn more about vehicles. The guide covers everything from the basics of how a car works to more advanced topics such as how to choose the right vehicle for your needs. It's the perfect resource for anyone who wants to learn more about vehicles, and it's free to download! To get your free copy of the "Ultimate Guide to Vehicles," simply enter your email address in the form below and we'll send it to you right away.

Once you have their contact information, you can begin converting them into customers. You can do this by sending them regular emails, offering them special discounts, or even inviting them to participate in your webinars or live events.

Now that you have a good lead magnet, the next step is to create an effective sales funnel. This involves creating several steps for potential customers to go through before they reach the final conversion. The initial step in your funnel should be to capture the attention of potential customers through an online ad, social media post, or email. Once they have taken up the offer, you can then direct them to a landing page where they can find more information and eventually make a purchase.

What is a Funnel and How Does it Work

A funnel is a marketing tool that helps you to focus your efforts on the most interested potential customers. It works by narrowing down the number of potential customers who see your product or service. This is done by targeting those most likely to be interested in what you offer. If you own an online store that sells handcrafted soaps, a great way to use a funnel is to offer a free sample of your soap to potential customers. This will help you to capture the attention of those most likely to be interested in your product and convert them into leads. You can do this by creating a lead magnet that offers a free sample of your soap. To create a successful free sample offer, you'll need to follow the steps outlined in this chapter. First, you'll need to identify the problem your soap solves and determine the audience you want to reach with your offer. Not only does this increase your online presence but it always allows you to build an email list to market your products to. Next, you'll need to create content that will interest potential customers and convince them to download your free sample. Finally, you'll need to promote your free sample on social media and other online platforms. If you follow these steps, you'll be able to increase traffic and sales for your online store!

The Benefits of Using a Funnel for Marketing

There are several benefits of using a funnel for marketing, including:

- Increased sales: A funnel can help increase sales by focusing your efforts on the most interested potential customers.

- Save time and money: By targeting only those most likely to be interested in your product or service, you can save time and money on marketing efforts.

- Improved customer engagement: A funnel can help to improve customer engagement by providing a more personalized experience.

- Easier tracking and measurement: The data collected through a funnel can track the success of your marketing efforts and measure the effectiveness of your campaigns.

How to create a funnel for your business.

- There are several steps involved in creating a funnel for your business, including:

- Identify your target audience: The first step is to identify your target audience, those who are most likely to be interested in what you offer.

- Create compelling content: The next step is to create content compelling and relevant to your target audience.

- Drive traffic to your content: The 2nd step is to drive traffic to your content so more people will see it.

- Convert leads into customers: The final step is to convert leads into customers by providing them with an excellent user experience.

There are several tips for using a funnel to increase sales, including:

- Offer something of value: The first step is to offer something of value to your target audience. This could be a discount, a free trial, or something else that would be appealing to them.

- Be clear and concise: It's important to be clear and concise in your messaging so potential customers know what you're offering and why they should choose you over the competition.

- Test and measure: The final step is to test and measure the results of your funnel so you can improve it.

Several examples of businesses using funnels successfully, include:

- Apple: Apple uses a funnel to drive traffic to its online store by offering free shipping on orders over $50.

- Amazon: Amazon uses a funnel to increase sales by offering discounts and coupons to customers who sign up for their Prime membership.

- Walmart: Walmart uses a funnel to drive traffic to its website by offering free shipping on orders over $35.

- Target: Target uses a funnel to increase sales by offering discounts and coupons to customers who sign up for their REDcard.

- Uber: Uber uses a funnel to increase the number of people using their app and improve customer satisfaction.

- Airbnb: Airbnb uses a funnel to increase website traffic and improve customer engagement.

Final thoughts on Funnels & Lead Magnets

Funnels and Lead Magnets are essential tools for any business looking to increase sales. In this chapter, we've provided a detailed look at what funnels are and how they work, as well as some tips for using them successfully. We've also outlined the benefits of using lead magnets to attract potential customers and convert them into buyers.

Finally, we've provided examples of businesses that are using these tools effectively to drive traffic and sales. If you want to increase your sales, it's important to implement a funnel and lead magnet into your marketing strategy. With the right strategy in place, you'll be able to maximize your reach and generate more leads, resulting in higher sales.

Chapter 16

When To Hire Someone To Market for Your Business

Sometimes, it makes sense to hire someone to help market your business. If you're struggling to keep up with the demands of marketing and don't have the time or resources to do everything yourself, then it may be time to bring on a marketing specialist. A marketing specialist can help you develop a marketing plan, create and implement marketing campaigns, and track the results. They can also help you identify and target your ideal customers and develop strategies to reach them. I mean now you know someone to hire....

There are a few things you should remember:

- What to consider before hiring a marketing specialist
- How to interview for a marketing specialist
- What to look for in a marketing specialist
- The benefits of hiring a marketing specialist

What to consider before hiring a marketing specialist:

Before you hire a marketing specialist, you need to consider your needs and budget. You also need to interview several candidates and ask them about their experience and what strategies they would recommend for your business. Get references and check them out. And finally, make sure the specialist is a good fit for your company culture.

How to interview marketing specialists:

When you're interviewing marketing specialists, ask them about their experience and what strategies they would recommend for your business. Also, ask them about their process for developing and implementing marketing campaigns, and how they track results. Get references and check them out. And finally, make sure the specialist is a good fit for your company culture.

What to look for in a marketing specialist:

When you're looking for a marketing specialist, you want someone with experience and who has developed successful marketing campaigns. You also want someone who is a good fit for your company culture and who you can trust to implement your marketing plan.

The benefits of hiring a marketing specialist:

There are several benefits to hiring a marketing specialist. They can help you develop and implement a successful marketing plan, reach your target customers, and track the results. They can take some of the burdens off you so you can focus on running your business. They can also free up your time so you can focus on other aspects of running your business. When you hire a marketing specialist, you're investing in your business. The main focus of having someone else focusing on this area of your business is to save you time.

Once you've found a marketing specialist you'd like to hire, here are the next steps:

- Evaluate your marketing efforts
- Look at metrics such as reach, engagement, leads, and sales
- Ask customers for feedback on their experience with your brand
- Test and experiment with new ideas

Marketing is an essential aspect of any business, and it should be evaluated regularly to determine what's working and what's not. There are several ways to evaluate your marketing efforts, including looking at metrics such as reach, engagement, leads, and sales. You can also ask customers for feedback on their experience with your brand. Finally, you should always test and experiment with new ideas to see what works best for your business.

Chapter 17

What the Future Holds for Online Marketing

The future of online marketing looks bright. With more people using the internet every day, businesses need to reach these customers through online channels. This is why online marketing will continue to grow in importance in the years to come.

This chapter discusses how technology will play a larger role in online marketing, and how businesses will need to adapt to stay ahead of the curve. It also explores new platforms and channels that will become popular, and how businesses can use them to reach their target audiences. One of the most popular platforms will be Snapchat and Tik-Tok, which offers a unique and interactive way to reach customers. Another channel growing in popularity is live streaming, which can give customers a behind-the-scenes look at your business. Whatever the future holds, it's important to keep up with the latest trends and find new ways to engage your customers.

Online marketing is always evolving. What worked yesterday might not work today, and what works today might be obsolete tomorrow. That's why it's so important for businesses to stay ahead of the curve and keep their finger on the pulse of the latest online marketing trends. Here are a few of the exciting things that the future holds for online marketing:

- Smarter Targeting: Thanks to advances in data collection and analysis, businesses can target their online marketing campaigns with unprecedented precision. No longer will businesses have to rely on broad demographics like age, gender, and location. Instead, they'll be able to target consumers based on their specific interests, behaviors, and even values.

- Increased Personalization: Along with smarter targeting will come increased personalization. Consumers will expect that their online experiences will be tailored specifically to them, and businesses able to deliver on this will reap the rewards.

- More Immersive Experiences: Thanks to developments in technology, online marketing will become more immersive than ever before. Virtual reality is already making its way into online marketing, and this trend will only grow in the years to come. Businesses can create interactive websites, videos, and other digital content. These technologies will allow businesses to create truly immersive experiences that will engage consumers on a whole new level: Augmented reality, virtual reality, and other cutting-edge technologies will allow businesses to create unique and engaging online experiences for their customers.

- Greater use of AI: Artificial intelligence is another technology starting to make its way into online marketing. AI-powered chatbots can already provide customer support and assist with sales, and this is only the beginning. AI will be used for even more complex tasks like creating personalized content and predicting consumer behavior.

- Automation: As online marketing becomes more complex, businesses will increasingly turn to automation to help manage their campaigns. Automation will allow businesses to free up time and resources so they can focus on other areas of their business. An example of a business that could use automation is a small business that does not have the resources to hire a full-time marketing staff. Automation tools can help manage and execute online marketing campaigns, freeing up time and resources for the business owner to focus on other areas of the business.

- Greater emphasis on ROI: With businesses under more pressure than ever to show a positive return on investment, the focus on ROI will only increase in the years to come. Online marketing campaigns will need to be carefully planned and monitored so businesses can see exactly how they are performing. With these advancements in online marketing, businesses will see a greater return on their investment. They'll be able to reach more consumers more effectively and efficiently than ever before, resulting in higher sales and profits.

- New platforms and channels: As online marketing evolves, new platforms and channels will emerge. It's important for businesses to stay ahead of the curve and experiment with these new platforms and channels so that they can reach their target audiences.

- Increased regulation: As online marketing becomes more widespread, it's likely that there will be greater regulation around certain practices, such as data collection and use. This could lead to changes in how businesses operate, but it will ultimately create a level playing field and ensure that consumers are protected.

- Increased spending: With more businesses competing for attention, marketing budgets will only continue to increase. This means there will be more money for businesses to invest in innovative and effective online marketing strategies.

- Greater Engagement: As online marketing becomes more targeted and personalized, engagement will increase. Consumers will feel like they connect with the brands they interact with online, leading to higher levels of brand loyalty.

- The Shift to Personalized Marketing: One of the most significant changes businesses will experience is the shift to personalized marketing. With more consumers using the internet to make purchasing decisions, businesses must tailor their marketing messages to individual consumers. This means that marketing will no longer be a one-size-fits-all approach, and each consumer will receive unique content tailored for them.

As the internet increasingly affects marketing, businesses must stay updated on the industry's latest changes. As online marketing evolves, businesses need to stay ahead of the curve. Your success is important to me! With each small step, you bring your online business one step closer to boosting sales significantly.

Online marketing is an ever-changing landscape. The future of online marketing is looking very positive, thanks to recent advancements in technology. The 11 changes that we've outlined will have a significant impact on the way businesses operate and market their products online. It's important for businesses to stay ahead of the curve and be aware of these changes so they can adapt their marketing strategies.

Here are some steps you can take to prepare your business for the future of online marketing:

Stay informed about new platforms and channels as they appear. Experiment with different platforms and channels to discover which works best for your business. Increase your spend on online marketing to stay competitive. Focus on ROI more than ever before to ensure that your campaigns are effective. Tailor content specifically for individual consumers based on their needs and preferences.

Make sure your website is mobile-friendly and easy to navigate. Increase investment in SEO to ensure that your site appears at the top of search engine results pages. Be prepared to follow new regulations around data collection and use. Keep track of changes in consumer behavior, so you can adjust your marketing strategies. Have a plan for how you will respond to negative feedback or criticism online. Take advantage of opportunities to connect with consumers on a personal level through social media and other channels.

Chapter 18
The Final Word

This is the final chapter, and it summarizes the key points covered throughout. Marketing is essential for businesses of all sizes, and there are many ways to market your business. You need to consider your target audience, your budget, and your goals when developing a marketing plan. There are also several channels you can use to reach your target customers including online, offline, and word-of-mouth. Finally, you should always test and experiment with new ideas to see what works best for your business.

- The importance of marketing
- Developing a marketing plan
- Reaching your target customers
- Testing and experimenting with new ideas
- The final word

The importance of marketing

Marketing is essential for businesses of all sizes, and it should be evaluated regularly to determine what's working and what's not. There are several ways to evaluate your marketing efforts, including looking at metrics such as reach, engagement, leads, and sales. You can also ask customers for feedback on their experience with your brand. Finally, you should always test and experiment with new ideas to see what works best for your business.

Developing a marketing plan

You need to consider your target audience, your budget, and your goals when developing a marketing plan. There are also several channels you can use to reach your target customers, including online, offline, and word-of-mouth.

Reaching your target customers

You can reach your target customers through online channels such as websites, social media, and email marketing. Offline channels include print media, direct mail, and telemarketing. And word-of-mouth is a powerful way to reach new customers.

Testing and experimenting with new ideas

You should always test and experiment with new ideas to see what works best for your business. This includes trying different marketing channels, different content formats, and different targeting methods.

The final word

This chapter summarizes the key points covered throughout the book. Marketing is essential for businesses of all sizes, and there are many ways to market your business. You need to consider your target audience, your budget, and your goals when developing a marketing plan. There are also several channels you can use to reach your target customers, including online, offline, and word-of-mouth. Finally, you should always test and experiment with new ideas to see what works best for your business.

What did you learn?

Chapter 1: Introduction

This chapter summarizes how marketing can help your business reach new customers and grow. It outlines the steps you need to take to create a successful marketing plan, include evaluating your current strategy, setting goals, targeting the right audience, and tracking results. Additionally, it provides tips for avoiding common marketing mistakes.

Chapter 2: Growing Pains with Marketing

The seven bad habits that can stand in the way of success are procrastination, perfectionism, analysis paralysis, fear of failure, fear of success, impostor syndrome and comparisonitis. These habits can be overcome with some self-awareness and a plan for change. *Overnight Marketing* is an effective way to quickly change your business for the better. It is a process that involves breaking down large goals into manageable steps and focusing on the progress you have made rather than the mistakes you have made.

Chapter 3: Your Method for Creating this Change

This chapter provides various tips on how to be more creative. This includes breaking rules, being open-minded, persistent, and flexible. It's also important to get enough sleep and keep your mind active.

You can do this by reading, learning new things, and taking on new hobbies. By following these tips, you can increase your chances of coming up with new ideas and being more successful in your business ventures.

Chapter 4: What Does Your Business Represent?

Decide what your business represents and stay true to those values. This will help customers connect with you and understand your message. Proper lighting can make a big difference to the overall look and feel of your space, which can translate into increased sales or foot traffic.

Make sure all bulbs are working at full capacity, take advantage of natural light, use accent lighting, and invest in quality lighting fixtures. Get creative with your lighting but be careful not to go overboard.

Chapter 5: Get More Customers in the Door

The five habits that stifle creativity are: being too focused, being afraid to fail, being a perfectionist, being too analytical, and being too rigid. To overcome these bad habits, you should try to be more flexible and open-minded. It's important to give yourself permission to make mistakes, take risks, and experiment with new ideas. It's also beneficial to break down large tasks into smaller ones that are easier to manage. Being a Perfectionist can be tackled by allowing yourself to make mistakes, set achievable goals, and revise your expectations. Tracking results is important to identify what works and doesn't work for your business. Being too analytical, can be addressed by taking a step back and looking at the bigger picture. The first step to overcoming these habits is to become more aware of them. Once you're aware of them, you can work on breaking them. Some simple steps to get you started including evaluating your current marketing strategy, trying new methods, starting small, tracking results, and celebrating successes. Additionally, it's important to stay up to date on the latest marketing trends to keep your business ahead of the competition.

Chapter 6: Increase Traffic to Your Business

This chapter provides eight steps to help increase creativity and ways to increase traffic to your business. Some key points include separating creation from evaluation, generating many ideas without judgment, and being persistent. Additionally, paid advertising can be an effective way to increase traffic to your website.

Chapter 7: The Power of Marketing

Come up with a plan that outlines your goals and objectives. Create content that aligns with those goals. Implement a distribution strategy that will reach your target audience. Stay up to date on the latest trends and changes in the industry. Consult professionals or other business owners if you need help.

Chapter 8: Marketing Your Business on a Budget

The main points in this chapter are that small businesses should set goals, use a social media strategy, and use paid advertising to reach new customers. Additionally, businesses should track their results to continue improving their marketing efforts. To summarize, businesses should focus on customer service, follow up with customers after purchases, and use marketing tools to reach new audiences. Additionally, businesses should track their progress to make the most of their marketing budget. With these tips, businesses can see real results from their marketing efforts.

Marketing your business does not have to break the bank. There are several cost-effective ways to reach new customers and grow your business. By setting goals, creating a social media strategy, and using paid advertising, you can reach new customers and build loyalty with existing ones. And don't forget to track your results so you can continue to improve your campaigns. With a little effort, you can see big results from your marketing efforts.

Chapter 9: Finding the Right Customer

To be successful in business, it's important to understand your target market and reach it with high-quality content. This could involve using a variety of marketing techniques to get your message out there. It's also important to be proactive and use various marketing techniques to reach your target market. Finding the right customers is essential for any business owner or marketing professional. By understanding your target market and writing a story that resonates with them, you can increase sales and traffic almost immediately. Get creative and try new things so you can stand out from your competition. Always be growing and expanding so you can keep up with changing trends.

Chapter 10: Online Marketing Techniques That Work

There are several things you can do to increase your online sales and traffic overnight including using relevant images, targeting your audience, using retargeting campaigns, and A/B testing your ads and landing pages. By following these tips, you can make your business more successful almost immediately. Implementing these changes will help you increase sales and traffic, and it will also help you build a more successful business overall.

Chapter 11: How to Get Your Business out into the Community

These tips include staying up to date on the latest marketing trends, reaching out to customers on social media, making it easy for customers to leave reviews, and following up with any leads. Implementing what you've learned is essential for seeing results. Remember that it takes time to see results from any marketing campaign—so don't give up overnight. Use tried and true methods that have succeeded for other businesses, but always be on the lookout for new strategies to try. With these tips, you can make the most of your time at local events and increase your chances of success. You'll be sure to have a successful event and turn those leads into customers.

Chapter 12: Business Ethics and Why They Matter More than Ever

One of the most important things to remember with business ethics is there are severe consequences for unethical behavior.

The penalties for this crime can be harsh, ranging from fines to imprisonment and long-term damage to your reputation. Additionally, unethical behavior can lead to a loss of trust from your customers which can have a devastating impact on your bottom line.

Unethical behavior can damage the business community. When businesses engage in dishonest or illegal practices, it makes the business community look bad. This can make it difficult for other businesses to succeed.

So, as you can see, ethical behavior is not only important for businesses but for the business community. If you want your business to succeed, you need to make sure you are always behaving ethically. There are a few things you can do to help ensure this:

Make sure that your values align with your actions. If you say you value honesty and integrity, make sure these values guide everything you do.

Be transparent in your dealings with customers. They should always know what they are getting from you, and never try to hide anything from them. Avoid any illegal or unethical behavior. This will only harm your business in the long run. Treat your employees fairly and with respect. They are an essential part of your business, and they deserve to be treated well.

Finally, make sure that you are always learning. The business world is constantly changing, and you need to make sure that you are keeping up with the latest developments.

Chapter 13: Telling Your Story

Telling your story is important for businesses as it helps customers connect with your brand and see you as more than a store. To tell your story effectively, make sure it is focused on the human element be genuine and authentic, and make sure it is reflected in your branding. When telling your story, focus on the positive aspects of your business to create a positive association with your brand. By following these tips, you can create a powerful story that connects with customers and builds loyalty for your business.

Chapter 14: Creating a Unique Selling Proposition

By remembering these key points, you can create a USP for your business that will help you stand out from the competition and increase sales. A strong USP is important for businesses today, as it allows you to differentiate yourself from your competitors. You can communicate your USP to potential customers in a variety of ways, such as through your branding, website, marketing materials, and sales pitches. There are many examples of successful businesses with strong USPs. Some of these include Apple, Amazon, and Southwest Airlines. Keep these key factors in mind when creating your unique selling proposition—focus on what sets you apart and communicate it in a way that is easy for people to understand and recall.

Chapter 15: Should You Use a Funnel for Marketing?

The content summarizes how funnels can increase sales and traffic to a business. It explains that funnels should be used with other marketing efforts and provides tips for how to create and use a funnel effectively. It also provides examples of businesses that have successfully used funnels to increase sales. Finally, it offers final thoughts on funnels and marketing.

Some key points to remember about using a funnel to increase sales are:

Offering something of value is the first step. Being clear and concise in your messaging is important

Test and measure the results of your funnel so you can improve it over time

Apple, Amazon, Walmart, Target, Uber, and Airbnb are all examples of businesses that use funnels effectively.

When using a funnel as part of your marketing strategy, remember that it should be just one element of your overall plan. To be successful, you need to focus on creating compelling content, driving traffic to your site, and converting leads into customers. By following these tips, you can use a funnel to increase sales and traffic to your business almost immediately.

Chapter 16: When to Hire Someone to Market for your Business

The key points of this chapter are to consider what you need before hiring a marketing specialist, how to interview them, and what to look for. Also, consider the benefits of hiring a marketing specialist. Once you've found a specialist you'd like to hire, follow these steps: negotiate the terms, finalize the hiring process, set up a meeting to discuss the marketing plan, implement the marketing plan, and evaluate the results.

Chapter 17: What the Future Holds for Online Marketing

There are some important changes that businesses need to be aware of when it comes to online marketing. These changes include the shift to personalized marketing, the increase in spending, and the rise of new platforms and channels. It's important for businesses to stay ahead of these changes and adapt their marketing strategies accordingly.

Now that you understand the basics of overnight marketing, it's time to act! Implement at least one tip from each chapter and see how your business changes. Remember, small changes can have a big impact, so don't be afraid to try something new. If you're looking for more in-depth information on these topics, check out our other resources. And as always, if you need help or have questions, our team is here to support you.

Additionally, it is essential to measure the success of your marketing efforts and avoid common mistakes. By following these steps, you can increase the chances of seeing success for your business through marketing.

Overnight Marketing is a method of transforming your business almost immediately through small changes in your marketing strategy. These changes can be easy to understand and implement, and by following the advice in this book, you can see a significant change in your business's success overnight. The concepts explained within these pages have been tried and tested by businesses of all sizes, and this guidebook provides valuable insight into how you can apply them to your own company. So, whether you're a small business owner looking for an edge over the competition, or a large corporation wanting to increase traffic, *Overnight Marketing* will show you how to get there.

Thank you for reading! I hope this guidebook provides valuable tips on how to market your business to make it more successful overnight. If you have questions, contact me. I'd be happy to help.

If you're ready to market your business overnight, here are the next steps:

1. Listen on **Overnight Marketing Tips Podcast** for new weekly marketing tips
2. Join the **Overnight Method** Facebook group and connect with other entrepreneurs
3. Follow and Like our social media pages

FB: armitagemarketing, Twitter: Armitagemedia, Instagram: armitagemarketing

Also, if you are looking for inspiration on your website or are interested in our services, check out armitagemarketing.com

Notes

Https://Blog.hubspot.com/Service/Customer-Service-Stats.